The Military Draft Handbook

Also by James Tracy:

*The Civil Disobedience Handbook: A Brief History
and Practical Advice for the Politically Disenchanted*

The
Military Draft
Handbook

A Brief History
and Practical Advice
for the Curious and Concerned

James Tracy
editor

Manic D Press
San Francisco

Dedicated to soldiers who question orders and youth who choose not to go to the military even though the rest of the world isn't offering them a whole lot...

...and to my father, who hated what he saw in Vietnam.

The Military Draft Handbook. Copyright ©2006 by Manic D Press, Inc. All rights reserved. Published by Manic D Press, Inc., PO Box 410804, San Francisco, CA 94141. www.manicdpress.com

Cover design: Scott Idleman/BLINK
ISBN 1-933149-01-9
Printed in the USA

Library of Congress Cataloging-in-Publication Data available.

"I just can't imagine it."

<blockquote>
— *Defense Secretary Donald Rumsfeld in response to the question: 'Under any circumstances, would a draft be necessary in the future?' (June 30, 2004)*
</blockquote>

"A free government with an uncontrolled power of military conscription is the most ridiculous and abominable contradiction and nonsense that ever entered into the heads of men."
— *Daniel Webster, speech in the House of Representatives, January 14, 1814*

Contents

The Military Draft Today

This is What a Draft Looks Like

What No Longer Works

What Continues to Work

Now What?

"The pioneers of a warless world are the youth that refuse military service." — *Albert Einstein*

What is the Draft?

Conscription — forced military service — is popularly known in the U.S. as The Draft.

The United States Armed Forces are composed of the Army, Navy, Air Force, and Marine Corps under the command of the United States Department of Defense. The Department of Homeland Security is in charge of the Coast Guard. Every state has a militia known as the National Guard, commanded by the state's governor and coordinated by the National Guard Bureau.

The President of the United States is Commander-in-Chief of all the armed forces. The President also has the authority to control individual state National Guard units.

In 1973, at the end of the Vietnam War, Congress abolished the draft in favor of an all-volunteer Army. Draft registration ended two years later in 1975 but was reinstated in 1980.

At least 27 nations require military service, including Brazil, Germany, Israel, Mexico, and Russia. At least 18 nations have volunteer armies, including Australia, Canada, Japan, the United Kingdom, and the U.S.

Who's in Charge of the Draft?

In between formal drafts, the Selective Service System functions as a massive information-gathering bureaucracy, ready to implement a formal draft should Congress and the President ever reinstate one. Within 30 days of turning 18, young men are supposed to register with the agency by filling out a brief postcard found at most post offices. After registration, Selective Service sends a "registration acknowledgment" letter, which repeats the information the registrant gave on the form and contains a Selective Service Number. This letter should be kept as proof of registration.

While the penalty for failing to register can be up to five years in jail and/or a fine of up to $250,000, it has been more than twenty years since anyone was prosecuted for failing to register, and no more than twenty people total have ever been prosecuted. Be aware that many states will not issue driver's licenses to those who evade registration, and non-registrants are also barred from receiving federal financial aid for school.

The Selective Service agency has five offices nationwide: a national headquarters in Virginia, a data management center in Illinois, and regional offices in Chicago, Denver and Marietta. At times, civilians may apply to become Local Board members. These individuals will ultimately decide which members of their community will enter the military, receive deferments, or qualify for Conscientious Objector (CO) status.

According to the agency, over 11,000 volunteers are currently trained in Selective Service regulations and procedures so that if a draft is reinstated, they will be able to fulfill their obligations fairly and equitably. Board members undergo an initial 8-hour training session and then participate in an annual training in which they review sample cases similar to real-life situations.

In 2003, an announcement on the SSS website soliciting new local board applicants made many fear that a formal draft was on the way. Actually, such notices are published annually as well as when membership declines. In the event of a formal draft, local board members may interview applicants for CO status individually and their decisions may be appealed to the Selective Service Appeals Board.

American Wars and The Draft

War	Draftees	Armed Forces Total
Civil War - Union Army (1983-1865)	164,000 (8%) inc. paid substitutes	2.1 million
WWI (1917 - 1918)	2.8 million (72%)	3.5 million
WWII (1940 - 1946)	10.1 million (63%)	16 million
Korea (1950 - 1953)	1.5 million (54%)	1.8M in country, 2.8M total
Vietnam (1964 - 1973)	1.9 million (56%, 22%)	3.4M in country, 8.7M total

A Brief History of The Draft

Before the 20th Century

Although conscription probably has existed since ancient times, it is generally acknowledged that modern conscription started in France in 1793 with *levée en masse*, the duty of all citizens to perform military service. To meet its defense needs, the Convention of the French Republic raised an army of 300,000 men through national service. France was followed by Sweden in 1812, Prussia and Norway in 1814, Spain in 1831, and Denmark in 1849. Conscription enabled the raising of mass armies without paying mercenaries, and altered the way wars are soldiered. Napoleon commanded the first mass conscription army of more than half a million French soldiers, which he led in battle against Russia in the late 1790s. Less than a hundred years later, the Northern German Alliance turned the tables and organized more than a million soldiers against France in the 1870s.

Early American History

"It must be laid down as a primary position and the basis of our (democratic) system, that every citizen who enjoys the protection of a free Government owes not only a proportion of his property, but even his personal service to the defence of it." — George Washington

The Constitution signed in 1789 gave Congress the "power to raise and support armies," but mandatory service was neither mentioned nor prohibited. Threats were few and far between in the early days of the U.S., and a two-army system evolved. The Regular Army, a small peacetime police force and wartime core unit, was created by voluntary enlistment. From the Indian Wars of the 1790s through the Spanish-American War of 1898, the volunteer soldiers were organized locally but federally financed and directed. Units of the so-called U.S. Volunteers were distinct from the U.S. Army and the militia, later called the National Guard.

Attempts to pass federal conscription laws for the War of 1812 failed, although some states legislated mandatory service.

During the Civil War in April 1862, the Confederacy adopted the draft. On January 1, 1863, President Lincoln issued the Emancipation Proclamation, which freed all slaves in the Confederacy.

President Lincoln declared, "There can be no army without men. Men can be had only voluntarily or involuntarily. We have ceased to obtain them voluntarily. The result is the draft."

Acknowledging an undersized military, Congress passed the National Enrollment Act in March 1863, which subjected all single men between age 20 and 45, and married men up to age 35, to a draft by lottery. Enlistment bonuses led to a large sector of impoverished men, namely immigrants and southern blacks, forming a sizeable portion of the Union army.

The draft was controversial, especially among the working class, because the wealthy could buy their way out by paying the government $300 (less than the cost of hiring a substitute, which was also allowable). In 1863, a mob burned the New York City draft office, touching off a five-day riot that targeted anger at the city's black population as well as the wealthy. The draft inductions resumed in August 1863, after the federal government stationed 10,000 soldiers in the city. Draft opposition occurred in other cities throughout the north, including Detroit.

World War I draft registration card
of Illinois farmer, age 23. 1917.

World War I

"Get together boys, and don't go. Rich man's war, poor man's fight. If you don't go, J.P. Morgan is lost. Speculation is the only cause of the war. Rebel now."

— Anti-conscription poster, WWI era

On May 18, 1917, the Selective Service Act was passed, authorizing the President to temporarily increase the military enrollment of the United States. The Selective Service System was responsible for the process of selecting men for induction into the military service, from the initial registration to the actual delivery of men to military training camps. Under the office of the Provost Marshal General, the Selective Service System was made up of 52 state offices (one for each of the 48 states; the territories of Alaska, Hawaii, and Puerto Rico; and the District of Columbia), 155 district boards, and 4648 local boards. These organizations were responsible for registering men; classifying them into how suitable each man would be for combat; considering needs for manpower in certain industries and agriculture; as well as the family situations of the registrants. These state, district and local boards also handled appeals of classifications; determined the medical fitness of individual registrants; determined the order in which registrants would be called; sent draft notices to registrants; and placed them on transportation to training centers. The federal government's Selective Service System is still in place today, using a similar model to the one implemented in WWI.

Less than a month after the Act was passed and signed into law, the draft was resurrected for the first time since the Civil War on June 5, 1917. This draft prohibited the enlistment bounties and personal substitutions that were allowed during the Civil War. It provided for religious conscientious objectors (COs) and was implemented through the Selective Service System. About three-quarters of the WWI army of 3.5 million was generated via conscription; slightly more than 10% of those who registered were called into service. The Civil War riots were not repeated, although there were protests.

Refusal, evasion, and occasional outright rebellion were common. At the time, many of those eligible for the draft were European immigrants, and many had extremely close ties with family members in their home European countries where World War I was being fought. Deferments were authorized on the grounds of supporting a family or essential work in industry or agriculture. Religious conscientious objectors (COs) could elect to take noncombatant roles within the military.

There were actually three draft registration periods for World War I. The First Draft (June 5, 1917) registered men between the ages of 21-31. The Second Draft (June 5, 1918) registered men who had turned 21 since the first registration; and the Third Draft (September 12, 1918) required all men, ages 18-21 and 31-45 (born between September 13, 1873 and September 12, 1900), to register who had not already done so. This was a significant proportion of the American male population. Twenty-four million men born between 1873 and 1900 registered in these three periods, and 2.8 million of them were drafted.

During the First World War, about 3 million men did not register, and 12% of those drafted never reported for service. In addition, 64,700 registrants sought Conscientious Objector (CO) status. Of the 20,900 COs drafted into the army, about 25% refused any sort of military activity.

Nationwide, No-Conscription citizens' groups flourished. These organizations agitated for Conscientious Objector classification for those opposed to war, and organized massive anti-war demonstrations. The anti-conscription movement's rise was aided by many of its key activists being prominent participants in the emerging labor and other populist movements.

One of the most dramatic acts of draft resistance was Oklahoma's 1917 Green Corn Rebellion, named for the time of year when the corn crop would first sprout. Entire communities, regardless of skin color or financial means, would take direct action by dispatching groups to destroy railroad bridges and cut telephone and telegraph wires, tear down fences and free farm animals to trample cotton fields to keep their areas free of military recruiters. They also faced vigilantes upset by the multiracial mutual cooperation of the rebellion.

Interestingly, the most intense anti-conscription activity went on in the rural South. Often deserters and resisters would flee to the hills, making a living through bootlegging alcohol. In stark contrast to today, much of the objection to the draft came from working-class people, while the educated urban population mostly supported the war.

REGISTRATION CARD—(Men born on or after April 28, 1877 and on or before February 16, 1897)

SERIAL NUMBER	1. NAME (Print)			ORDER NUMBER
U *1442*	*Mimka*	*Johnson*	*Habben*	
	(First)	(Middle)	(Last)	

2. PLACE OF RESIDENCE (Print)

R. 4.   *Carthage*   *Hancock*   *Illinois*

(Number and street)   (Town, township, village, or city)   (County)   (State)

[THE PLACE OF RESIDENCE GIVEN ON THE LINE ABOVE WILL DETERMINE LOCAL BOARD JURISDICTION; LINE 2 OF REGISTRATION CERTIFICATE WILL BE IDENTICAL]

3. MAILING ADDRESS

SAME

(Mailing address if other than place indicated on line 2. If same insert word same)

4. TELEPHONE		5. AGE IN YEARS		6. PLACE OF BIRTH
		60		*Hancock,*
		DATE OF BIRTH		(Town or county)
		11 *11* *81*		*Illinois.*
(Exchange)	(Number)	(Mo.) (Day) (Yr.)		(State or country)

7. NAME AND ADDRESS OF PERSON WHO WILL ALWAYS KNOW YOUR ADDRESS

Mrs. Tjode Habben.

8. EMPLOYER'S NAME AND ADDRESS

Self.

9. PLACE OF EMPLOYMENT OR BUSINESS

Carthage   *Hancock*   *Ill.*

(Number and street or R.F.D. number)   (Town)   (County)   (State)

I AFFIRM THAT I HAVE VERIFIED ABOVE ANSWERS AND THAT THEY ARE TRUE.

Mimka Habben

D. S. S. Form 1   (Revised 4-1-42)   (over)   16—21630-2   (Registrant's signature)

World War II draft registration card of
60-year-old man from Illinois, April 1942.

World War II

After France fell to Germany in 1940, Congress enacted a pre-war ("peacetime") draft; conscripts only had to serve one year. During World War II, public opinion widely accepted the fight against Hitler to be crucial, and combat against Japan an absolute necessity after the bombing of Hawaii's Pearl Harbor. Given the intensity of the times, many who opposed World War II set aside their objections to military service. President Franklin Roosevelt signed the Selective Training and Service Act of 1940 which created the country's first peacetime draft and formally established the Selective Service System as an independent Federal agency. So many men were drafted during WWII — 10.1 million which made up 63% of the entire U.S. armed forces at the time — that in April 1942, the U.S. conducted a fourth draft registration for men between the ages of 45 and 65. Though never called to serve, these men were in the oldest age group ever required to register with the Selective Service System.

Objection to war came from various perspectives. Some people were deeply suspicious of American motives for entering the war, as businesses including Ford Motor Corporation, General Motors, and Chase Manhattan had openly supported Nazi Germany with the trade of weapons and other goods. Isolationism — the idea the U.S. should stay out of all foreign conflicts — was an extremely popular political concept and expressed mainly by veterans of World War I who had experienced the devastating effects of war firsthand.

Most of the draft resistance of this era came from populations that were truly against all wars — the historic peace churches — the Brethren, Mennonites, and Quakers. Only about 12,000 people applied and received Conscientious Objector status. Many participated in the Civilian Public Service Program, performing alternative duties at mental hospitals, factories, and Conservation Corps camps nationwide. About ten million were drafted, and 43,000 soldiers refused to fight. Nearly six million men voluntarily enlisted, primarily in the U.S. Navy and Army Air Corps. The federal government imprisoned 6,000 men who resisted conscription and documented 350,000 cases of draft evasion.

These numbers paint a more complicated picture than the one most commonly portrayed in popular culture — that of a war whose sanctity was universally accepted. The most well-known example of draft resistance in the World War II era was the case of the Union Eight, a group of Union Theological Seminary students who refused orders to register with the Selective Service. The draft started as a peacetime draft, since the United States had not yet entered the war in 1940. Every individual in the Union Eight, as religious students, could have gained automatic CO status, yet chose prison to dramatize their objection to war.

Of the 72,000 registrants who applied for CO status, 25,000 entered the army in noncombatant service, another 12,000 went to civilian work camps, and 20,000 had their claims rejected. Imprisoned were 6,000 resisters, many of who were Jehovah's Witnesses. Some anti-draft incidents in Chicago and other cities stemmed from protest by African-Americans against discrimination and segregation in the armed forces. The Justice Department investigated 373,000 draft evaders and convicted 16,000.

The Union Eight and peace activists of this era certainly had little effect on World War II, but the organizing skills honed during this time prepared them for pivotal roles in the emerging civil rights and anti-nuclear movements. Bayard Rustin spent a year on a Southern chain gang for draft resistance and later became one of the key architects of the non-violent direct action campaigns associated with the work of Dr. Martin Luther King. World War II objectors created the Pacifica radio network, and pushed for humane reforms in the mental institutions where many performed their alternative service. Organizations such as the War Resisters League, the Congress of Racial Equity, and the Fellowship of Reconciliation came of age during this time as well, and continue to this day to participate in anti-war work.

On December 24, 1947, after the war had ended, President Harry S. Truman pardoned all wartime draft resisters.

The Case of WWII Japanese-American Draft Resistance

In 1944, 63 young men, all American-born citizens of Japanese descent, stood trial for resisting the draft at the internment camp at Heart Mountain, Wyoming. Seven leaders were accused of conspiring to encourage them. They were convicted and spent two years in prison.

In December of 1941, World War II was already raging in Europe, but the Japanese attack on the naval base at Pearl Harbor still stunned the American public and drew the nation into the war in the Pacific. This attack against the U.S. by Japan cast governmental suspicion on all persons of Japanese ancestry in the U.S., and came on top of a century of anti-Asian prejudice and discriminatory laws. Despite being warned there was no military necessity, and having no evidence of planned sabotage or imminent invasion, President Franklin D. Roosevelt ordered 110,000 persons of Japanese ancestry from the West Coast to ten American prison camps in seven states: California, Wyoming, Idaho, Utah, Arizona, Colorado and Arkansas. They held both the Issei, first-generation immigrants who were barred from U.S. citizenship, and their children, the Nisei, born in this country as U.S. citizens. Two-thirds of those forced to the camps were U.S. citizens.

When Tak Hoshizaki decided to fight his draft notice in 1944, he figured he had a pretty strong legal case. For two years, the 18-

year-old L.A. native had been held at the Japanese-American internment camp in Heart Mountain, Wyoming. The U.S. government had labeled his parents "enemy aliens" and imprisoned his entire family behind barbed wire. Federal law exempts prison inmates from the draft until after they are released. After all this the U.S. government wanted to draft him?

"According to their own rules, you can't draft people out of prison," Hoshizaki remarked. He found out otherwise. "As soon as the judge started calling us 'Japs', I figured we'd had it," he recalled. He was right. Hoshizaki was convicted of draft evasion and spent the next two years in a federal penitentiary in Washington State.

On June 12, 1944, 63 Japanese-Americans stood trial for draft evasion in Federal Court in Cheyenne, Wyoming. It is the largest mass trial in Wyoming history. Two weeks later, the resisters were convicted and sentenced to three years in a federal penitentiary. Twenty-two more were later convicted, bringing the total number of resisters from Heart Mountain to 85. On July 14, 1946 nearly all the draft resisters at the McNeil Island, Washington federal penitentiary were released with time off for good behavior.

Korean War

Both the Korean and Vietnam Wars were fought within relatively small geographical boundaries, unlike WWII which covered vast areas of Europe and the Pacific region.

While WWI, WWII, and the Korean and Vietnam Wars were actively fought on battlefields, in the air and at sea, the Cold War between the U.S. and the former Soviet Union (of which the largest territory was Russia) was ongoing following the end of WWII until the demise of the Soviet Union in 1991. The Cold War was a war fought because of ideas (Capitalism vs. Communism) with no physical combat between the U.S. and the Soviet Union. Instead, it was a war of threats, spying, propaganda, arms buildups, and lies. Indeed, the U.S. feared the Soviets' Communist influence along many borders around the world, and America had to meet several simultaneous global military commitments.

During the Korean War era, only 1.6 million Americans actually fought in the war zone though more than 4 million soldiers served worldwide. That 73% majority, whether drafted or enlisted, was put into uniform to combat communism in two distinct areas — Asia and Europe. Because of the Cold War, hundreds of thousands of GIs would have served in Germany and other parts of Europe between 1950 and 1953 even if there had not been combat in Korea.

On March 12, 1947, America officially declared "war" on Soviet Communist expansion in Europe. The Truman Doctrine proclaimed containment. "Europe First" was the center of America's post-WWII defense strategy. The peacetime draft was renewed on June 24, 1948—two full years before the Korean War erupted.

An army, four air forces, and a fleet of ships were all mobilized to protect Europe from the perceived threat of the Soviet Union. In 1951, four Army divisions were sent to Germany to bolster NATO against the hostile Soviet Union. NATO, the North Atlantic Treaty Organization (also known as the Western Alliance), was formed after WWII on the principle that an armed attack against one or more countries in Western Europe or North America would be considered an attack against them all. By 1954, 352,644 U.S. troops were stationed in Europe—50,000 more than were on the ground in Korea at war's end. All of these military moves would have been made, regardless of Korea. Some 1.7 million men were drafted during the Korean War era.

In the United States, the conflict in Korea was termed a police action under the auspices of the United Nations rather than a war, in order to circumvent the requirement of a Congressional declaration of war.

In the Korean War, despite the employment of eight National Guard divisions, it was necessary to turn to the draft, calling up as many as 50,000 men per month. CO cases accounted for about 1.5% of those conscripted. 80,000 draft evasion cases were investigated, although few actually came to trial. In 1952, 7,777 men were registered with the Selective Service as Conscientious Objectors.

Vietnam War

Given that the reinstitution of the draft during the Vietnam-era produced massive protests and spread anti-war sentiment into the mainstream, it would be easy to conclude that the bulk of enlistees during this war were drafted. In reality, draftees made up only about 16% of the entire American armed forces. However, by 1968, draftees comprised about 88% of infantry riflemen and therefore represented the bulk of the battlefield deaths.

The draft helped to build an unlikely coalition of organizations working to end the war, uniting churches, campus activists, feminists, civil rights and radical groups. Break-ins to destroy files at draft boards, mass demonstrations, and public burning of draft cards by the young men who received them were frequent as the anti-war movement experienced great public notice through the unifying factor of the draft.

Between 1964 and 1973, of the 26.8 million draft-aged men, over 60% did not serve in the military. Legal exemptions or deferments were given to 15.4 million, and approximately 570,000 evaded the draft illegally. Among draft evaders, 8,800 were convicted, and 4,000 sent to prison. About 360,000 were never caught, and another 198,000 had their cases dismissed. In previous wars, it was only possible to obtain Conscientious Objector status through religious objections. The Supreme Court in 1970 added ethical and moral considerations to the CO definition as well. Between 1965 and 1970, 170,000 registrants were classified as COs.

December 1, 1969 marked the date of the first draft lottery held since 1942. This drawing determined the order of induction for men born between January 1, 1944 and December 31, 1950. A large glass container held 366 blue plastic balls containing every possible birth date. A ball was chosen randomly and each birthdate announced in a live television and radio broadcast.

On January 27, 1973 — the day the Vietnam ceasefire was announced — the administration stopped the draft, six months earlier than the draft law was to expire on July 1, 1973.

Disproportional amounts of deferments given to middle-class young men characterized the Armed services during the Vietnam War. Black Americans, while only being 11% of the entire U.S. population, comprised 28% of the combat troops, accounted for 16% of the army's casualties in Vietnam in 1967, and 15% for the entire war. One out of every two Latinos who went to Vietnam served in a combat unit. In 1970, Latinos made up 27% of the population in New Mexico but supplied 69% of all those drafted in the state.

Within the anti-war movement, the difference between a Conscientious Objector (CO), a Resistor, and an Evader became very acute. Many felt that declaring oneself a CO played into the military's agenda by weeding out those who would make poor soldiers, and in some cases by accepting alternative non-combat assignments in the military that enabled others to kill. Many were concerned that the majority of CO claims granted by local draft boards went to middle-class young white men affiliated with peace churches like the Quakers while blacks, Latinos, and poor whites were shipped off to fight. Resistors were very publicly burning draft cards and refusing induction. Evaders left for Canada, got letters from their doctors declaring them unfit to serve, or stayed in college to keep deferring a draft notice. Most of America didn't recognize a difference between them, labelling them all "draft dodgers."

Many felt that the only moral choice was to refuse to cooperate with the Selective Service in any way. It became common for potential inductees to publicly burn their draft cards at demonstrations, or quietly refuse to register. Often resistors would spend time in federal prison, serving terms of up to four years. 250,00 avoided draft registration and one million committed draft offenses. Of 25,000 formally indicted who openly resisted the draft, 3,250 went to prison.

At the same time that domestic resistance to the draft was at an all-time high, enlisted people, many of whom were already in the combat zone, made the war unmanageable for the brass. Acts of refusal, civil disobedience, and outright mutiny became widespread in the final years of the war.

In 1970, the Army had 65,643 deserters, an amount roughly equal to the population of an averaged-sized North American suburb. "Search and avoid" missions were frequent as soldiers deliberately walked away from potential battles and often hid for days far away from the battlefield. Once, on CBS-TV, the Air Calvary Division refused to advance down a treacherous trail. Previously, the 196th Light Infantry Brigade conducted a sit-in on the battlefield.

Demonstrations often turned into riots at military bases. In one situation, threat of a full-scale mutiny forced the aircraft carrier USS Constellation back to port in San Diego. Direct Action and sabotage on more than one occasion halted boats from sailing altogether. On the USS Anderson, someone dropped chains, bolts, hardware and nuts down the main gear shaft. In a scene reminiscent of the Boston Tea Party, sailors once threw vital equipment overboard.

Interview with Drafted Vietnam Vet Richard Tracy

Describe your background growing up.

I grew up in a very different Berkeley, California than what most people think of when they think of that city, not a hotbed of radical activity. Both of my parents were workers. My father drove a truck for the Teamsters, and my mother worked at the old Hink's Department store on Shattuck Avenue. We had a large Italian-American family; my grandparents were immigrants to this country.

When were you drafted? How were you notified?

I was drafted in 1966, after I had graduated from college and started a teaching assignment. The school district did all kinds of things to help me out when I got drafted, but I had to work two days and write out all of the curricula in advance for the Substitute Teacher. The sub in the room was there observing for those first two days. I was notified the same way everyone else was, by a draft notice. I hadn't received a notice while I was in college so, of course, I never sought a deferment.

I had taught 4th grade for a year and a half before I was told to report for induction in January. I tried to get a deferment once I got the letter. The principal at the school wrote a letter on my behalf and said that I was needed at the school but that didn't work. I got the feeling that all they wanted at the Induction Center was a warm body.

At the time it seemed as if everyone was getting a notice. My cousin Bob got one, but was excused because he had asthma. My cousin David was in the Seminary at the time so he didn't have to serve.

One thing that gets me really angry today is the Stop-Loss orders for those serving. They are really a backdoor draft in my opinion. One of the things that got me through my time was that I knew it would be over with. If I survived my time in Vietnam, I would come back home, do some time at an Army base then be discharged. These National Guard types are really in a bad way. I do think that people should know that before they enlist in the Guard or the Reserves that there is a chance they are going to get called up. You are in the service, you are collecting a paycheck and you might be called into combat.

What was the induction center like?

You felt as if they had a quota — they were going to pass you any way they could! I measured very high blood pressure so they made me lay down on a cot for an hour to bring it down to normal. I remember having to go through all sorts of tests. They qualified me there to be a Clerk-Typist. Given my eyesight, how I qualified for that I'll never know.

What was your initial emotional response? Did you want to go?

I was petrified! Of course I didn't want to go to war. I was scared and part of me wanted to run away. I had managed to complete college without getting drafted, and thought I was out in the clear because I had started a teaching career.

I think that having started a career before I was drafted made me aware of what I had to lose. If I had run to Canada, like some people did, then I wouldn't have been able to return home. I would not have been able to see my family again or teach class. Because I had some education behind me, I was constantly being "encouraged" to train to be an officer; and constantly being chewed out when I told them No. I told the Army that if I got out of Vietnam alive I would be very happy to go back to the U.S. and teach class. Had I become an officer, I don't know how long I would have had to stay there.

Did any of your friends or family go?

No. There was one guy, Gary Weaver, from my area who I became friends with in Basic. I didn't have very many friends in Vietnam. Jim Spencer, my next door neighbor, joined the Navy and did missions in Vietnam.

What was it like being in a war zone in Vietnam?

I always tell people that you don't really know until you have been there; always in a paranoid, heightened state of alert.

How did you adjust when you got back?

Much more easily than many people. I returned to the same community that I left, and they were very supportive of me. I got letters while I was in Vietnam from people who were my age or older, and they welcomed me back when I got home. For the first five or six years after I returned, I had horrible nightmares about Vietnam, especially every February, which was the month I got out. I got out just as the Tet Offensive was beginning in 1968. I got very close to being killed in my last week there.

I was at an airbase getting ready to send my dog, Gina, who I had adopted in Vietnam, back home. I was sleeping outside with my dog tied up, and all around us on the ground were metal caskets filled with dead soldiers. All of them were full. It was outside of a white trailer. A nurse asked me if I would come inside. All night there were just grenades and grenades coming over. All it would have taken was one to get under the trailer and I would have been done for.

How do you feel about the military today?

I'm not anti-military, really. I am, however, against wars that are based on deception and lies. The country needs some sort of military but Iraq has very little to do with defending people who live in the United States from terrorism.

As a retired educator, how do you feel about the provisions of the federal No Child Left Behind Act that require schools to turn over student records to military recruiters?

First of all, the parts of No Child Left Behind that don't have anything to do with the military are horrible in and of themselves. It is as if whoever wrote it forgot some of the most basic parts of good teaching: that children learn and grow in different ways. The law was passed right after I retired but teachers I know who are still working hate it. However, I think that the government still has too much access to personal information, and sharing student records with recruiters does not make any sense. The school is a school, and students should be able to study and learn without a recruiter contacting them.

Do you support opt-out efforts?

Of course I do. Every parent and student should be informed of their rights to keep this information from recruiters.

As a veteran critical of the government, do you regret your decision to go to war?

No, I regret the government's decision to send us there. I'm the type of person that will try to make the best out of the worst situation. At the time I didn't have enough information to make an informed decision. I hated the idea of war, but had nothing to help me decide that the government was lying about why we were there. While I was there, I tried to also work relief efforts. I organized my entire family to send relief packages for the Montagnards—a group of indigenous people living in Vietnam that were getting it from all sides, highly discriminated against by all levels of society.

Do you ever think about going back to Vietnam?

Yes. I would like to go back and work with the Vietnam Friendship Village near Hanoi. They build schools and work with the victims of Agent Orange and chemical warfare. I send them money about three times a year, but I would like to return, this time in peace.

Editor's note: A retired educator, Richard Tracy lives in Fairfield, California. He's also my father. As a young parent, he always tried to keep war toys out of the house because his Army service left him with a deep disgust of violence. It was a memorable occasion when he took the toy guns that went with 'Star Wars' action figures out of our hands and told my brothers and me that we needed to find peaceful solutions.

Chicano Moratorium

On August 29, 1970, with cries of 'Raza si, guerra no' ('Our people, Yes—War, No'), more than 25,000 U.S.-born citizens of Mexican descent marched down Whittier Boulevard in Los Angeles to demand an end to the Vietnam War. This was the largest protest ever organized by Chicanos in the U.S. The march was dubbed the 'Chicano Moratorium' to call attention to the disproportionate amount of Chicanos fighting and dying in Vietnam. At the time, men of Mexican heritage constituted about 6% of the population but about 20% of the battlefield casualties.

The march culminated in what is now Salazar Park in East Los Angeles. This important demonstration was remarkable in that prior to the Vietnam War, military service was seen as a path for improving economic conditions and helping Latinos gain acceptance into mainstream white society. The Los Angeles Police Department aggressively attacked the marchers, killing three people including *L.A. Times* journalist Ruben Salazar.

The Chicano Moratorium was significant in the political growth of Los Angeles' Latino community and a signal that opposition to the draft and war was growing considerably. The turmoil of the Vietnam War fueled many other upheavals in North American society including the organizing drives throughout the Chicano community that centered around farm workers in rural areas, while urban activists turned their attention towards police brutality, full employment, and building a self-determined base of political autonomy.

Interview With Drafted Vietnam Vet Victor Haney

When were you drafted?

I went in January 1970, even though I always considered myself a Conscientious Objector. At that time, I wasn't even a novice activist, all I knew was that I hated the war, it didn't make sense and I didn't want to go. I had received numerous draft notices in the mail and I had always managed to avoid the induction, telling them I was ill, or just not showing up. Then one day I was in Compton and I received a letter from my mother and in the envelope there was a final warning letter from the Selective Service so I had to report to the induction center.

What was your reaction?

I was petrified, simply scared and didn't know what to do.

Did you consider dodging, going to Canada, or burning your draft card?

Not seriously. Where I grew up you didn't have peace churches coming in to educate us on what the alternatives were. I grew up in California's Central Valley, in public housing. In my community it was like the civil rights movement never happened. I got on the bus, went back to Stockton to say goodbye to my mother then took the bus to the Induction Center.

What was the Induction Center like?

It was big, I remember a big brown building with an American flag flying from on top of it. We went in, they basically said you are in the Army now and made us swear the oath to defend the country against all enemies. They told us we would be defending the country against all communists, and I didn't even understand what a communist was. They didn't go into any great lengths telling us what a communist was, what his thinking was, what his ideology was. It was just that a communist was an enemy to the United States; they hated our freedom. I didn't understand how Vietnamese people were going to get over here to take over our country—but that is what they were telling us was going to happen.

But you applied for Conscientious Objector status anyhow?

Yes, and ultimately I was given an alternative assignment, as a staff clerk in Saigon. It didn't seem like much of an alternative, since I was on the same battlefield as everyone else basically. For me, it was saying that I didn't mind helping my country in some way but I wasn't going to take someone's life for it, at least not in this way.

They would ask us if we would go to any length to defend our country, any length to defend our freedoms and they seemed like trick questions. I wasn't being asked to defend my country or my freedoms at all. I was being asked to invade someone else's. I didn't see any connection between defending my home and being in Vietnam.

But actually, I was granted CO status pretty easy, perhaps because I was willing to serve out my time in Vietnam, I don't know.

SELECTIVE SERVICE SYSTEM

**ORDER TO REPORT FOR
ARMED FORCES PHYSICAL EXAMINATION**

Approval Not Required.

LOCAL BOARD NO. 8
FEDERAL BUILDING
1000 LIBERTY AVE.
PITTSBURGH, PA. 15222

(Local Board Stamp)
FEB 6 1970
(Date of mailing)

To

JOHN DOE
123 MAIN ST.
ANY TOWN, PA 15222

SELECTIVE SERVICE NO.
36 | 8 | 50 | 665

You are hereby directed to present yourself for Armed Forces Physical Examination by reporting at:

ASSEMBLY ROOM - 17th FLOOR. FEDERAL BLDG.
1000 LIBERTY AVENUE PITTSBURGH PA.

(Place of reporting)

on FEB 18 1970 at 7 A.M.
(Date)   (Hour)

(Member, Executive Secretary or clerk of Local Board)

IMPORTANT NOTICE
(Read Each Paragraph Carefully)

TO ALL REGISTRANTS:

When you report pursuant to this order you will be forwarded to an Armed Forces Examining Station where it will be determined whether you are qualified for military service under current standards. Upon completion of your examination, you will be returned to the place of reporting designated above. It is possible that you may be retained at the Examining Station for more than 1 day for the purpose of further testing or for medical consultation. You will be furnished transportation, and meals and lodging when necessary, from the place of reporting designated above to the Examining Station and return. Following your examination your local board will mail you a statement issued by the commanding officer of the station showing whether you are qualified for military service under current standards.

If you are employed, you should inform your employer of this order and that the examination is merely to determine whether you are qualified for military service. To protect your right to return to your job, you must report for work as soon as possible after the completion of your examination. You may jeopardize your reemployment rights if you do not report for work at the beginning of your next regularly scheduled working period after you have returned to your place of employment.

IF YOU HAVE HAD PREVIOUS MILITARY SERVICE, OR ARE NOW A MEMBER OF THE NATIONAL GUARD OR A RESERVE COMPONENT OF THE ARMED FORCES, BRING EVIDENCE WITH YOU. IF YOU WEAR GLASSES, BRING THEM. IF YOU HAVE ANY PHYSICAL OR MENTAL CONDITION WHICH, IN YOUR OPINION, MAY DISQUALIFY YOU FOR SERVICE IN THE ARMED FORCES, BRING A PHYSICIAN'S CERTIFICATE DESCRIBING THAT CONDITION, IF NOT ALREADY FURNISHED TO YOUR LOCAL BOARD.

If you are so far from your own Local Board that reporting in compliance with this Order will be a hardship and you desire to report to the Local Board in the area in which you are now located, take this Order and go immediately to that Local Board and make written request for transfer for examination.

TO CLASS I-A AND I-A-O REGISTRANTS:

If you fail to report for examination as directed, you may be declared delinquent and ordered to report for induction into the Armed Forces. You will also be subject to fine and imprisonment under the provisions of the Military Selective Service Act of 1967.

TO CLASS I-O REGISTRANTS:

This examination is given for the purpose of determining whether you are qualified for military service. If you are found qualified, you will be available, in lieu of induction, to be ordered to perform civilian work contributing to the maintenance of the national health, safety or interest. If you fail to report for or to submit to this examination, you will be subject to be ordered to perform civilian work in the same manner as if you had taken the examination and had been found qualified for military service.

SSS Form 223 (Revised 9-29-65) (Previous printings may be used until exhausted.)

Order to Report for Physical Examination letter (1970)
sent to men prior to being inducted
in the 1969 draft lottery during the Vietnam War.

The following article appeared in newspapers the day after the 1969 draft lottery; December 2, 1969.

Sept. 14 'Wins' Draft Lottery

***

June 8 Brings Up The Rear; 850,000 Affected by Drawing

By Mike Miller

WASHINGTON — The Selective Service System today was notifying the nation's 4,000 draft boards to arrange their files of draft eligible young men for 1970 with those born Sept. 14 at the top of the heap to be called up first.

And the official notice sent to state and local Selective Service authorities places those men with June 8 birthdays in 366th position — at the very bottom.

850,000 Involved

That was the start and the finish of last night's long-awaited lottery-by-birthday drawing, which opened with an invocation and closed with a benediction.

In between it saw the draft future being determined for an estimated 850,000 young men, many of whom must have been saying their own prayers about the results.

For those with birthdays drawn in the upper portion of the lottery list — April 24, Dec. 30, Feb. 14, Oct. 18, Sept. 6, Oct. 26, Sept. 7, Nov. 22 and Dec. 6 round out the top 10 — the uncertainty over their draft status has ended.

Plans Can Be Made

They now know they will be drafted early in the year unless they volunteer first. And those at the bottom know that they will not be drafted and can plan their lives accordingly.

For those in the middle or marginal area of the drawing, uncertainty still exists. But they certainly will know definitely by the end of 1970 whether they will be inducted.

They would have had a maximum of seven years of uncertainty under the old system of drafting first the oldest available men age 19 through 25. This system expires Jan. 1.

Drawing Low-Key

The lottery was conducted in low key fashion with young men and women representing Selective Service's youth advisory committees in the various states drawing capsules containing slips of paper with the birth dates on them from a water-cooler size glass bowl.

Rep. Alexander Pirnie, New York Republican who drew the first date, was the only person in an official capacity to pull out the capsule. Mr. Pirnie is the senior Republican on the House Armed Service Committee's special subcommittee on the draft.

More Reform Urged

But the use of the young people led to a few public expressions of dissent that while the lottery is commendable, more wide-ranging draft reforms should follow.

Three young men expressed such sentiments while a fourth, David L. Fowler representing the District of Columbia, said he had been "notified" not to draw and walked out. Nevertheless, Lt. Gen. Lewis B. Hershey, 76, Selective Service director who has been accused of heavy-handed draft policies, rose and shook Mr. Fowler's hand.

About a dozen youthful demonstrators picketed outside, denouncing the draft, the lottery and the Vietnam war, but they failed to interfere with the smooth precision of the drawing.

Following the drawing of dates, including Feb. 29 for men born in a leap year, the young people also drew the 26 letters of the alphabet to determine the order for induction for men registered with the same draft board and having the same birthday. J was drawn first, V last. Thus a man named Jones would be drafted before Vickery under those circumstances.

Upon receiving official notice of the lottery's results, local draft boards will arrange their files of registrants accordingly and draft in the order dates were drawn. After a board has filled its draft quota for the year, those men whose birthdays have not been reached will be free of all draft liability except in time of extreme national emergency.

As a general rule, Selective Service expects those with dates drawn in the upper third of the list will be drafted. Those in the middle third are of questionable status and those in the bottom third will not have serve.

The estimated 850,000 who will be 19 through 25 and classified 1-A or draft eligible as of Jan. 1 are directly affected by last night's drawing. After the first year, only men 19 at the beginning of the year and older men with deferments which have expired will be affected by the annual lotteries.

For men now in the 19-25 pool with college or other deferments, the position their birthdays were drawn will determine their liability in the year their deferments expire. For example, President Nixon's son-in-law, David Eisenhower, apparently will be ripe for drafting when his deferment expires in mid-1970 upon his expected graduation from Amherst College. His birthday, March 31, was drawn 30th. Since men in the 30th position in his draft board probably will already have been drafted by June, David would go to the top of his draft board's list of eligibles.

Neither Gen. Hershey nor any of the other Selective Service officials present moved to cut off the statements of the handful of participants who spoke out. Larry McKibben, the Iowa representative, read a petition he said represented the views of 14 young people. The 14 objected to the barring from the proceedings of Michigan and Alaska delegates who had come to Washington for the occasion but then reportedly announced they would refuse to draw out birth dates. John M. Bowers of Minnesota said the petition did not represent the views of any of the others.

*　*　*　*　*　*　*

Note: In reality, the lottery numbers of 19-year-old men were called at a rate of 30 per month, at least for the early 1970 months of January through May. For example, a man with a number of 131 was ordered to report for his physical exam on February 18, 1970, subsequently classified 1-A, and then ordered to report for induction May 20, 1970 (May's maximum quota allowance called men with the numbers 121 through 150).

The draftee with the number 131 was in the Central Highlands of Vietnam by February of 1971 at his first duty station, following Basic Combat Training (BCT) and Advanced Individual Training (AIT) at Ft. Dix, New Jersey.

The highest number drafted in this group of men was 195.

SELECTIVE SERVICE SYSTEM

Approval Not Required.

ORDER TO REPORT FOR INDUCTION

The President of the United States,

To

JOHN DOE
123 MAIN ST.
ANY TOWN, PA 15222

LOCAL BOARD NO. 8
FEDERAL BUILDING
1000 LIBERTY AVE.
PITTSBURGH, PA. 15222

(LOCAL BOARD STAMP)

APR 23 1970

(Date of mailing)

SELECTIVE SERVICE NO.

| 36 | 8 | 50 | 665 |

GREETING:

You are hereby ordered for induction into the Armed Forces of the United States, and to report
ASSEMBLY ROOM - 17th FLOOR, FEDERAL BLDG
at .... 1000 LIBERTY AVENUE, PITTSBURGH, PA. ....

(Place of reporting)

on MAY 20 1970 at 7 A.M.

(Date) (Hour)

for forwarding to an Armed Forces Induction Station.

M. F. Gallo

(SIGNATURE, Executive Secretary, or Member of Local Board)

IMPORTANT NOTICE
(Read Each Paragraph Carefully)

If you are so far from your own local board that reporting in compliance with this Order will be a serious hardship, go immediately to any local board and make written request for transfer of your delivery for induction, taking this Order with you.

IF YOU HAVE HAD PREVIOUS MILITARY SERVICE, OR ARE NOW A MEMBER OF THE NATIONAL GUARD OR A RESERVE COMPONENT OF THE ARMED FORCES, BRING EVIDENCE WITH YOU. IF YOU WEAR GLASSES, BRING THEM. IF MARRIED, BRING PROOF OF YOUR MARRIAGE. IF YOU HAVE ANY PHYSICAL OR MENTAL CONDITION WHICH, IN YOUR OPINION, MAY DISQUALIFY YOU FOR SERVICE IN THE ARMED FORCES, BRING A PHYSICIAN'S CERTIFICATE DESCRIBING THAT CONDITION, IF NOT ALREADY FURNISHED TO YOUR LOCAL BOARD.

Valid documents are required to substantiate dependency claims in order to receive basic allowance for quarters. Be sure to take the following with you when reporting to the induction station. The documents will be returned to you. (a) FOR LAWFUL WIFE OR LEGITIMATE CHILD UNDER 21 YEARS OF AGE—original, certified copy or photostat of a certified copy of marriage certificate, child's birth certificate, or a public or church record of marriage issued over the signature and seal of the custodian of the church or public records; (b) FOR LEGALLY ADOPTED CHILD—certified court order of adoption; (c) FOR CHILD OF DIVORCED SERVICE MEMBER (Child in custody of person other than claimant)—(1) Certified or photostatic copies of receipts from custodian of child evidencing serviceman's contributions for support, and (2) Divorce decree, court support order or separation order; (d) FOR DEPENDENT PARENT affidavits establishing that dependency.

Bring your Social Security Account Number Card. If you do not have one, apply at nearest Social Security Administration Office. If you have life insurance, bring a record of the insurance company's address and your policy number. Bring enough clean clothes for 3 days. Bring enough money to last 1 month for personal purchases.

This Local Board will furnish transportation, and meals and lodging when necessary, from the place of reporting to the induction station where you will be examined. If found qualified, you will be inducted into the Armed Forces. If found not qualified, return transportation and meals and lodging when necessary, will be furnished to the place of reporting.

You may be found not qualified for induction. Keep this in mind in arranging your affairs, to prevent any undue hardship if you are not inducted. If employed, inform your employer of this possibility. Your employer can then be prepared to continue your employment if you are not inducted. To protect your right to return to your job if you are not inducted, you must report for work as soon as possible after the completion of your induction examination. You may jeopardize your reemployment rights if you do not report for work at the beginning of your next regularly scheduled working period after you have returned to your place of employment.

Willful failure to report at the place and hour of the day named in this Order subjects the violator to fine and imprisonment. Bring this Order with you when you report.

SSS Form 252 (Revised 1-23-50)   (Previous printings may be used until exhausted.)

Order to Report for Induction letter (1970) sent to men
drafted in the 1969 draft lottery during the Vietnam War.

Draft Lottery Story by Don Allcock

The upcoming day when the lottery would take place hung over us unlike any upcoming final. We had our cars packed and were ready to hit the road to Canada should our birthdays come up early in the draft. Boyhood friends of our family had moved to Canada ten years prior and settled in Montreal. That was my first destination if my luck ran out.

On the day of the lottery, the five of us who rented that house in Dayton, Ohio while we attended the University of Dayton sat with an enormous amount of trepidation. Nobody talked. We were all way too nervous. As the birthdays were called, we sighed an enormous sigh of relief as each date passed that wasn't ours. Inevitably, however we did know some acquaintances whose birthdays came up in the first 100. Nothing was said then either. We all knew the common acquaintances, and the personal ones we suffered quietly. Only one of us didn't make it out of that first 100. Ed retreated out to the porch and silently cried. There was not much we could do to comfort him. He was not one of those who felt comfortable moving to Canada.

When the first 100 passed, we again felt an enormous burden lifted off our shoulders, but we were still not out of the woods. However, as each date passed and we moved closer to 200 we were able to breathe easier date by date. When they hit 200 and we still weren't called, we went out and got the drunkest I've ever been in my life. I couldn't believe the weight that was lifted off my shoulders.

The Amazing Case of Heavyweight Boxing Champion Muhammad Ali

In April 1960, when he turned eighteen, professional boxer Ali (still known as Cassius Clay) registered for the draft in Louisville, Kentucky. In March 1962, Ali was classified 1-A, eligible to be drafted. Two years later, just weeks before he won the heavyweight boxing title from Sonny Liston, he failed the pre-induction mental examinations. Ali scored in the sixteenth percentile, far below the thirtieth percentile score required to pass. A second mental test proved that Ali did not fake the first exam, and he soon received a classification of 1-Y, not qualified for service. The publicity that followed his deferment humiliated Ali. "I said I was the greatest," he told reporters, "not the smartest."

In early 1966, as the demand for troops increased, the Army lowered its standards on the mental exam to make anyone with a score in the fifteenth percentile or better eligible for the draft. In March, Ali's local draft board reclassified him 1-A. The heavyweight champ couldn't understand it and, in frustration, uttered the famous words: "Man, I ain't got no quarrel with them Vietcong." On August 23, 1966, Ali petitioned the Selective Service to obtain CO status on religious grounds as a member of the Nation of Islam. His request was denied.

By the time he refused induction in 1967, he had become so controversial that he was stripped of his license to box and his heavyweight champion belt, and was sentenced to five years in prison. Ali filed an immediate appeal and was released on bond. The sentence was overturned three years later, by a Supreme Court unanimous decision.

Ali did not fight again until 1970. He gave up the best years of his remarkable athletic career for his refusal to be drafted.

From Generation to Generation:
An Interview with Kate Berrigan

Some of the most persistent anti-draft actions in the Vietnam War era were led by the Berrigan Brothers, Daniel and Philip, a pair of Catholic priests who linked the fight against war abroad and poverty everywhere. Philip Berrigan took radical action on October 27, 1967 when he and three other men broke into the U.S. Customs House in Baltimore and poured fresh blood on draft record files, destroying government property in the process. After his arrest, Phil read a statement charging that "America would rather protect its empire of overseas profits than welcome its black people, rebuild its slums, or cleanse its air and water. We invite our friends of peace to move from dissent to resistance."

Seven months later, while out on bail for the Baltimore action, Phil, Dan and seven other clergy and former clergy raided the draft offices in Catonsville, Maryland and destroyed 378 Selective Service files.

Rather than go to prison, the Berrigan Brothers went underground. Both Berrigans became prolific writers while on the lam. Later, in prison, Philip secretly married Sister Elizabeth McAlister, a fellow activist, which resulted in their excommunication from the Catholic Church.

After being paroled in 1972, both brothers continued their non-violent actions with "Plowshares" protests at weapons plants. They were repeatedly arrested and imprisoned, and continued to write prolifically. Philip's daughter, Kate Berrigan, continues to organize against war and poverty. At 23, she carries the torch of her family and keeps strong links with today's counter-recruitment and anti-war work.

Kate, is it still important to have a religious component in the anti-war counter-recruitment movements?

Secular and religious social justice folks have more in common than people often realize. Catholic anti-war activists are often motivated by an understanding that U.S. empire-building in an era of total war can never be defined as "just war." Implicit in this understanding, though, is the fact that these continual wars are most devastating not only to the poor abroad, but to the youth of color and poor youth who are targeted for recruitment in the U.S.

What anti-draft tactic do you think is most closely associated with your family?

Catonsville Nine, an action in 1968 in which my father, uncle and seven others burned hundreds of draft files, comes first to many people's minds when the name Berrigan is mentioned. In 1980, though, Phil and Dan with six others began the Plowshares movement, which involves symbolic disarmament of nuclear weapons with hammers and participants' own blood.

My mother, Elizabeth McAlister, spent two and a half years in prison for a Plowshares action when I was very young. Through the years, members of Jonah House, the anti-war resistance community where I grew up, have been at the core of the Plowshares movement, and there have been over 80 Plowshares actions worldwide.

Has there been much connection between the anti-draft activists of the 1960s and today's counter-recruitment efforts?

I think connections are being made among people working against militarism — but both generations could put more energy into it. In my experience, many folks doing counter-recruitment work today are young folks of color with deep anti-colonialist, anti-imperialist politics, working in their own communities where military recruiting is most intense. In contrast, many older, white folks who were active in the Vietnam War era and are still doing anti-war work today have trouble making connections with local poverty or racism work already happening, and thus supporting those who are hardest hit by war and recruitment.

For me, one of the most powerful things about the work of my parents and others in the Catholic left has continually been the clarity and conviction their faith gives them. Not descending into dogma, rather constantly pushing them to follow their hearts and consciences while loving, respecting and being open to others, even opponents — this faith provides a grounding for community, for discernment, for action. Young folks and secular folks find that in other ways; I think communities of support, education, reflection are essential, whether faith-based or not.

Any thoughts on the call for the return of a formal draft with the argument that it is preferable to the economic one we have now?

Progressives, people who oppose war, the draft, or simply government theft for war of resources we need to live, need to loudly, strongly, and consistently oppose any draft, any war. Over the past year or so there has been much debate over the Democratic migration towards the right. I believe that the more compromises we make, the more we allow the whole country to move further to the right. Instead of justifying a "formal draft" by claiming it's more truthful, let's name the draft already in place: an economic draft, a poverty draft, a war on people of color and poor people.

The Military Draft Today

Code Red: High Anxiety

With the formal draft legislation currently defeated in Congress, why does draft anxiety persist? It's simple. For the first time, an American President has pursued a war that he admits might never end. This war requires additional ground occupations against a backdrop of declining military recruitment and retention, and military desertions.

There are approximately 1.2 million active duty soldiers in the Army, Navy, Air Force, Marines, and Coast Guard. The Army's commitments include about 130,000 troops in Iraq, 11,000 in Kuwait, 11,500 in Afghanistan, 37,500 in South Korea and 44,000 in Japan. Currently, the United States has more than a million troops stationed in 141 countries around the world.

In 2005, signs emerged of the military's current recruiting crisis. The Army fell more than 6,700 recruits below its goal of 80,000 for the year that ended Sept. 30, 2005. It was the first time it had fallen short since 1999, and the largst shortfall since 1979. In March, the Army Reserves raised the maximum age of enlistment to 39. And the Army is allowing more enlistees who score in the bottom third of those tested to be accepted into the military. Those who score the lowest on the aptitude test — less than 30 points out of a possible 99 — are known as Category IV. The test quizzes potential soldiers on general science, mathematics and word knowledge. Since 1990, the number of Cat IVs has been 2% or under. Currently, the number is 4% and may grow.

For 2005, the Army fell under quota by 8%, its Reserves by 16%, and the Army National Guard by 20%. This is in spite of the fact that the active-duty Army added nearly 1,300 recruiters during 2005, for a total of 6,401 as of Sept. 30, and the Army Reserve added nearly 600, for a total of 1,547 recruiters. These recruiters spend an average of $14,000 per recruit, from a total $3 billion departmental budget.

Damien Cave wrote in *The New York Times*, "The Army is seeking 101,200 new active-duty Army and Reserve soldiers this year alone to replenish the ranks in Iraq and Afghanistan, elsewhere around the world and at home. That means each of the Army's 7,500 recruiters faces the grind of an unyielding human math, a quota of two new recruits a month, at a time of extended war without a draft."

Kathy Dobie, in *Harper's* magazine, observed, "The Pentagon has estimated that since the start of the current conflict in Iraq, more than 5,500 U.S. military personnel have deserted..." Thirty-seven of these desertions have been from Military Recruiters, frustrated with a very difficult job.

The Draft paradox may be the trickiest one for military strategists to maneuver around. On one hand, formal drafts throw once-popular wars into the trash-heap of public opinion. The federal government, mindful of Vietnam, has every strategic reason to avoid one. Yet the All-Volunteer Army (AVA) system is at its breaking point and an aggressive foreign policy of additional ground occupations without an exit strategy is nearly impossible without an on-going influx of new soldiers.

A formal draft is dangerous to the war-making politicians' interests at home (for example: they'd like to be re-elected, and/or have their party in control of the White House and Congress). However, it may become necessary for war-making politicians to reinstate a draft to accomplish their stated global aims (of establishing democracy and a capitalistic economic system in other countries).

The Return of the Draft?

Elected politicians understand that a formal draft would galvanize voters' opposition to the war; and will do just about anything to avoid one. The Vietnam-era draft brought anti-war sentiments out of the counterculture and into the mainstream. For this reason, a formal draft may not be around the corner, but let's explore several very possible scenarios that could lead a nation back to conscription.

1) Recruiters will first ascertain that no additional bodies can be squeezed from public housing developments, trailer parks, minimum wage strip-malls, high schools, undocumented farm workers, and unemployment lines. This 'Poverty Draft' must have reached its limits. This may already be the case, given the ongoing inability of the Armed Forces (including the National Guard) to meet their recruiting goals.

2) The 'Backdoor Draft' executed through "stop-loss" orders that hold service people in a hellish limbo of on-going extended duty will have to be no longer useful.

3) Under serious consideration is the possibility of a limited 'Special Skills Draft' in which those with medical, high tech, or foreign language translation skills could be conscripted. Also being considered is the recruitment of non-Americans into the armed forces, though this service would more likely be called a

Freedom Legion rather than a Foreign Legion.

4) Forced conscription (a formal draft) is the fourth phase of military recruitment. A formal Military Draft is a mandatory conscription of individuals into the Armed Services in time of war or national emergency. The ability to implement such a draft efficiently comes from the requirement that all men must register with the Selective Service System within thirty days of their eighteenth birthday. The Selective Training and Service Act of 1940 created the country's first peacetime draft. Drafts have nearly always been used to fill gaps in manpower needs when "voluntary" enlistment has fallen short.

This is What a Draft Looks Like

A future formal draft could very likely be different from past drafts. However, it is likely that the process of implementation will be very similar to past ones.

The resurrection of a draft must be established through legislation. It's possible that a state of emergency could accelerate the legislative process, as demonstrated by 2001's USA-Patriot Act which was written, approved by Congress and signed into law by the President in less than six weeks. According to the Selective Service website, "A lottery based on birthdays determines the order in which registered men are called up by Selective Service. The first to be called, in a sequence determined by the lottery, will be men whose 20th birthday falls during that year, followed, if needed, by those aged 21, 22, 23, 24 and 25. 18-year-olds and those turning 19 would probably not be drafted."

As in past drafts, those with low lottery numbers will be required to report for a physical, mental, and moral assessment at a Military Entrance Processing Station. Those deemed eligible would have ten days to file a claim for deferment, exemption or postponement.

Currently, potential enlistees may be classified as such:

1-A: available immediately for military service.

1-O: Conscientious Objector — conscientiously opposed to both types (combatant and non-combatant) of military training and service — fulfills his service obligation as a civilian alternative service worker.

1-A-O: Conscientious Objector — conscientiously opposed to training and military service requiring the use of arms — fulfills his service obligation in a noncombatant position within the military.

2-D: Ministerial Students — deferred from military service.

3-A: Hardship Deferment — deferred from military service because service would cause hardship upon his family.

4-C: Alien or Dual National — sometimes exempt from military service.

4-D: Ministers of Religion — exempted from military service.

Local and Appeal Boards will be set up to process registrant claims. Once induction orders are received, the law allows ten days to report for duty.

Phase I: The Poverty Draft

An Armed Services made up of volunteers is commonly referred to as an "Economic Draft." Such a draft occurs when one turns to enlistment to obtain housing, education, healthcare, and steady income. The majority of those in the military are poor whites from rural areas. However, military recruiters are aiming to change that, returning the military's demographics to Vietnam-era diversity. They are adding hip-hop concerts and tricked-out black Hummer sport utility vehicles to the usual appeal of chances for economic advancement.

Today's relatively low level of recruits of color can be traced in part to the anti-recruitment organizing of the '60s. Efforts such as the Chicano Moratorium, Muhammad Ali's refusal to fight, and the activism of returning GIs created a culture of refusal among draft-aged men.

Anti-war activist Aimee Allison observed, "Recruiters receive intense training on how to market themselves to low-income youth. It is sales training, like a used car dealership. They are trained to always ask themselves, 'What can I tell a teenager?' They can provide gifts and take the kids out, something that youth might not have in everyday life. Part of the marketing is the reminder, 'Hey, you matter!' Again, something that youth might not have in their everyday life."

Sergeant First Class Jemahl D. Martinson, a military recruiter from Oakland, California, does not deny that culture and marketing are being used to brand the military into the minds of urban youth. "Marketing, that's what we do. We identify our target and audience, and identify common threads. It is like selling cars or ads in the phone book. We use culture to do this. We sponsor the AM1 Tour that features a lot of physical and athletic stars along with a lot of youth-oriented music. We also have another approach called *The Centers of Influence* where we target adults who have contact with youth. We cosponsored the Anthony Hamilton tour. He is an R&B singer who has a very Afro-centric vibe. The idea is very simple: get exposure, let people know what we do. We want these adults to talk to youth about how joining the military is a good option for them."

In order to appeal to urban youth, the Armed Forces have turned to an unlikely partner: the hip-hop industry. The Army, together with the premiere national hip-hop magazine *The Source* co-sponsored the "Campus Combat" tour featuring well-known hip-hop artists such as Nappy Roots, Black Moon, and Memphis Bleek.

Recruiters and counter-recruiters are locked in a pitched battle using the exact same cultural weapons. While the military co-sponsors concerts with *The Source* magazine featuring big-name acts, counter-recruitment organizations such as AWOL, a project of the venerable Central Committee for Conscientious Objectors (CCCO), counter-attack with an underground, yet extremely well-produced magazine of the same name. Every issue comes with a free CD that combines politically-charged music from unsigned acts along with tracks from Spearhead, The Coup and others.

According to *DMZ*, a zine put together by activist youth, "The military's recruitment drought over this past year has led them to seek newer and more innovative means of recruiting. Several hip Navy commercials directed by Spike Lee appeared last year during the NBA playoffs. The cast was primarily black and Latino. It was no secret that Spike was chosen because "he's able to connect us to an audience we're interested in recruiting," according to Navy spokesman Edward Brownlee.

"Indeed, Latinos particularly are the new target population of military recruitment efforts. They have been referred to as an 'untapped goldmine.' The same old promises of money for education, job opportunities and other lies are being recycled to the new 'culturally sensitive' killing machine."

Kevin Ramirez is a staff organizer for AWOL. In addition to producing the magazine *DMZ*, the job entails a lot of direct organizing on high school and college campuses. "In Philadelphia, where I'm based, they have JROTC in more than eight high schools in almost every neighborhood of the city. They have a JROTC at West Philly High School as well as a recruiting station there. They have their main recruiting station in downtown Philly, then another one in North Philly and one in the Cheltenham Mall in the Cheltenham section of Philadelphia. They have a large JROTC unit in Germantown High School and just this year they opened a public military academy at Leeds Middle School available for 9th graders."

Allison places the economic draft in a broad political context: "I start with the assumptions that the schools are being basically choked off through decades of budget cuts and that every child deserves a school that can help her or him grow into a full human being. Art and music are being looked upon as extras or unnecessary. The facilities are crumbling, our schools are staffed largely by inexperienced teachers. This leaves an opening for the recruiters to fill: they target the bright students who would otherwise stay after school in clubs and extracurricular activities." During the 2004-05 school year, Allison's hometown of Oakland, California shut down seven public schools.

Ramirez is quick to point out that a just economy is bad for the military. "Economic injustice is what drives many people to enlist in the first place. When there are more job opportunities in America, you have fewer people enlisting in the armed forces. Even the military will own up to the fact that when the economy is good, it's bad for recruiting."

Sergeant Martinson doesn't completely disagree. "I saw the movie 'Fahrenheit 9/11'. There were some points in it that I disagreed with, but I couldn't argue with the point that it is poor people who do the fighting. When [director Michael] Moore was going around asking the Congresspeople if they would send their kids to war, I thought, *Good point*. We all know who is going to war."

When asked whether he would rather have his budget for recruitment doubled or Jenna Bush joining the military, he replied, "I already have had my budget doubled! Jenna Bush, of course. But let's face it, if Jenna Bush goes into the military, we know she's not going anywhere near Iraq. Draft or no draft, rich people know how to keep their kids out of combat."

Mario Hardy, the Third World Outreach Coordinator for the Central Committee of Conscientious Objectors wrote in the 1999 issue of *AWOL*: "If there were one place where there is more likelihood of encountering a U.S. military presence than the rundown city streets of any Third World country, it would be the impoverished communities of color right here in the United States. The old slogans — "Aim High!", "Be All You Can Be",

"The Few, The Proud,...", and "Go Navy!" — have entrenched themselves into the daily realities of people of color throughout America's urban battlefields. Yes, these are the same battlefields that instruct African-American youth to "Just Do It!" while assuring them that Colt 45 "Works Every Time"; the same playing field on which the U.S. encourages young Latinos to "Just Say No!" while extending an open invitation to "Come to Marlboro Country". Exactly like its counterparts in the fashion, alcohol, drug, and cigarette peddling rackets, the U.S. military is concentrating its efforts on attracting young people — and, as usual, young people of color are its most desired commodity.

"In 1999, recruiters are making unprecedented efforts to lure Third World youth into the lowest ranks of the military. Latino youth comprise the most sought-after group of prospective recruits in the land. For the past year, Secretary of the Army Luis Caldera has been trotting around the country, invading inner-city schools and telling tales of unlimited opportunity for Latino youth in the armed services. If careers in the military are a world of opportunity for Latino youth, why does it continue to hold true that only 3% of commissioned officers are Latino, as compared to whites who make up 81% of officers? While being grossly underrepresented in the officer corps, Latinos have historically been overrepresented in one crucial area: casualties in war. An overwhelming 28% of the names on the Vietnam Memorial in Washington, D.C. are Latino."

African-American recruits are an equally hot commodity. The Navy paid $2.5 million to filmmaker Spike Lee to aid in their mission of tracking low-income youth of color. Interestingly, Navy officials pull no punches as to why Lee, the director of "Malcolm X" and "Do the Right Thing", was chosen: he's hip and he's cheap. The bid that he submitted was the lowest of any received for this campaign.

What ended the Vietnam War was the government realizing that their soldiers would no longer fight the war, not only because of how the war transformed these soldiers but also due to the very visible and passionate anti-war movement in the U.S. and around the globe. In anti-war organizing and activism, we have reached the equivalent of six years in Vietnam after two years at war in Iraq. As more and more soldiers get killed and maimed for life physically and mentally, the anti-war effort will grow by numbers, and tactics will diversify. Participating in counter-recruitment work nips militarism in the bud and engages young people in a way that brings them into a movement — before they have to learn about war's brutality the hard way as many will on the streets and sands of Iraq.

Within the ranks of the military recruiters there is considerable anxiety about bringing back a formal draft. Many career soldiers and officers are actually opposed to it. "We don't want to go back to the days of Vietnam with massive desertions, fragging [the killing of officers by enlisted people], people cutting their meat so they couldn't fight, etc. That is exactly what you get with a draft," remarked Martinson.

Fact: The Bill of Rights only applies to civilians. Military personnel do not enjoy freedom of speech or privacy, and do not have the constitutional right to a "speedy and public trial, by an impartial jury."

Fact: Fewer than 50% of veterans receive GI Bill money for college.

Fact: 1 out of every 4 homeless men is a veteran.

Phase II: The Back Door Drafts —
Stop Loss and Stop Movement Orders

Imagine that you are in the U.S. military. After a tour in Iraq, your service contract is just about up. You begin to make plans to return to civilian life, back to family, school or a career. Then the orders come in. You're not going anywhere. You have been the recipient of a stop-loss order.

In the Iraq war, stop-loss orders have become one of the main strategies for ensuring that there will be enough troops for a continued occupation. According to federal regulations, in any conflict when soldiers have been called to duty the President "may suspend any provision of law relating to promotion, retirement or separation applicable to any member of the armed forces who the President determines is essential to the national security of the United States." All of the Army's combat units and most of its Marine units were deployed to Iraq or Afghanistan in 2003 or 2004. Most soldiers have experienced at least one rotation or 'stop-loss' order since the invasion of Afghanistan; and about one-fourth of all ground-force Reservists have been mobilized since 9/11/01.

The "stop loss" orders force enlisted people who could otherwise leave the military to remain in service, often in a combat zone, for up to another 90 days after their obligations are complete. In addition, "stop movement" orders also bar soldiers from taking on new assignments during the restricted period. For example: someone serving active duty in Iraq who might otherwise be eligible to transfer back to the U.S. for the remainder of their obligation would not be allowed to do so.

The military has had stop-loss capability since the Vietnam War. In preparation for the Gulf War, the practice was reinstated in 1990. The policy of stop-loss has been called a "back door draft" by many observers, an attempt to try to avoid a formal draft through this and the deployment of reserve troops. Another law also allows almost all retired regular or reserve military personnel to be ordered back to active duty. There are currently 9-10,000 soldiers under stop-loss orders.

"It is a giant upheaval for military families. Stop-loss messes with the future. They were expecting their loved ones to come home, to retire, to go back to school, to find a job. Stop-loss orders messes all that up," remarked Joyce Raezer of the National Military Families Association. "The solutions are simple: create a bigger Army or take on fewer missions. The Army has more missions than what it can do at one time."

Phase III: The Special Skills and Medical Draft

The military is actively pursuing the idea of instituting a Special Skills and Medical Draft, as shown by the following notes of a meeting held February 11, 2003 between the Department of Defense and the Selective Service System.

...Defense manpower officials concede there are critical shortages of military personnel with certain special skills, such as medical personnel, linguists, computer network engineers, etc. The costs of attracting and retaining such personnel for military service could be prohibitive, leading some officials to conclude that while a conventional draft may never be needed, a draft of men and woman possessing these critical skills may be warranted in a future crisis.

In line with today's needs, the SSS' structure, programs and activities should be reengineered toward maintaining a national inventory of American men and (for the first time) women, ages 18 through 34, with an added focus on identifying individuals with critical skills.

An interagency task force should examine the feasibility of this proposal which would require amendments to the MSSA [Military Select Service Act], expansion of the current registration program, and inclusion of women. In addition to the basic identifying information collected in the current program would require all registrants to indicate whether they have been trained in, possess, and professionally practice, one or more skills critical to national security or community health and safety. This could take the form of an initial "self-declaration" as part of the registration process. Men and women would enter on the SSS registration form a multi-digit number representing their specific critical skill ... taken from a lengthy list of skills to be compiled and published by the Departments of Defense and Homeland Security. Individuals proficient in more than one critical skill would list the practiced skill in which they have the greatest degrees of experience and competency, they would also be required to update reported information as necessary until they reach age 35. This unique database would provide the military ... with immediately available link to vital human resources ... in effect, a single, most accurate and complete, national inventory of young Americans with special skills.

There are long-standing plans for a medical draft that are currently on hold. Like a formal draft, a medical draft would have to be approved by Congress and the President. According to the Selective Service System, the medical draft would "provide a fair and equitable draft of doctors, nurses, medical technicians and those with certain other health care skills if, in some future emergency, the military's existing medical capability proved insufficient and there is a shortage of volunteers." Deferments would be available based on one's necessity in their home community.

Phase IV: A Possible Formal Draft

Draft "experts" tend to fall into two camps. One swears that a formal draft is right around the corner, and sometimes distorts mundane government documents as "proof" that it is coming, in much the same way that Chicken Little's sky was falling. The other denies that possibility altogether, ignoring the very real recruiting and retention crisis the military is now experiencing.

Early on in the planning stages of the Iraq War, the military reasoned that the war with Iraq would not last long enough to require a draft. Iraq's infrastructure had been decimated by the previous Persian Gulf War and a decade of economic embargo. In fact, some government documents imply that the Bush Administration had anticipated a "Get in, get out" situation. Shortly after the Iraq election, talk of "exit strategies" have been replaced by "success strategies" — an indirect way of saying we really don't know when the troops are coming home.

According to an Associated Press report on Oct. 19, 2005, members of the Senate Foreign Relations Committee asked Secretary of State Condoleezza Rice specifically whether the U.S. would have troops in Iraq in five or ten years. Rice replied that it would not be appropriate for her to speculate on how long troops will remain in Iraq. The Secretary of State also did not rule out the use of military force against neighboring Syria and Iran.

Although the Bush Administration has publicly said it opposes a draft, the sheer mathematics of war and occupation suggest otherwise. Many insiders are predicting an occupation of Iraq and Afghanistan that will last for many more years. Should another country come into U.S. crosshairs, such as Iran, Syria or North Korea, the tipping point of starting a formal draft will be well past.

If the United States occupies only Iraq and Afghanistan, it is likely that it will try to go without a formal draft. During the Vietnam War era, massive conscription led to massive resistance, far beyond what the Pentagon thought was manageable dissent. The draft helped to convince much of Middle America, the "silent majority" which President Nixon asserted was for the war, not to be so silent.

However, an on-going occupation combined with other confrontations, such as North Korea or Iran, greatly increases the possibility of a formal draft. Shortly after President Bush's second inauguration, the Associated Press reported that the administration was seriously considering the invasion of Iran. Chris Toesing, in *The Progressive* magazine, established that although opinion in government circles is split on the matter, regime change in Iran remains a high priority for many close to the President while some in Congress are agitating towards yet another war in the Middle East.

In July 2005, Republican Senator Rick Santorum of Pennsylvania introduced a bill calling upon "the United States to support regime change for the Islamic Republic of Iran and to promote the transition to a democratic government to replace that regime." The bill did not pass out of committee, but Santorum reportedly plans to reintroduce it again in Congress. Senator Sam

Brownback, Republican from Kansas, crows on his website about having slipped a provision for "not less than $3 million to support the advancement of democracy and human rights in Iran" into the Omnibus Appropriations Bill passed in November 2004. Similar measures continue to incubate in the House of Representatives.

Other possible targets are Syria, which the U.S. has blamed for training terrorists and encouraging Iraqi resistance, and North Korea, for continuing to develop their nuclear capabilities. However, the determining factor could be a good deal less dramatic than a new invasion: plummeting military recruitment fueled by increased casualties in Iraq.

Early in the latest Iraq conflict, Washington analysts estimated only several hundred U.S. casualties and several thousand wounded. With the death and casualty toll well above that mark, one crucial requirement for the resumption of the draft has already been met. Enlistment naturally drops with an increased number of reported deaths and casualties.

A simple formula for a formal draft: continued occupation in Iraq and Afghanistan, plus soldiers leaving the military by the bundle, with additional invasions and occupations. With tens of thousands of Reservists having been involuntarily activated multiple times in the War on Terror, it is obvious that the recruiting crisis could intensify soon.

Discussion of the return of a draft has been influenced by several political factors: the hard, cold numerical requirements of the Army which as the nation's largest service needs more recruits than other branches like the Marines, Air Force, and Navy; occupation and possible invasion of additional nations; a social conservative notion of "national service"; and the new liberal notion that a draft would promote social equity and spread the human cost of war across class and race lines.

What No Longer Works

The Canadian Non-Option?

More than 50,000 draft-age Americans went to Canada during the Vietnam years, according to professor John Hagan. About half of them remain in Canada even though President Jimmy Carter pardoned them in 1977.

Nowadays, some of the people fleeing deployment in Iraq — Specialist Jeremy Hizman, Brandon Hughey of the Army's 1st Calvary, and David Sanders of the Navy — are finding that it is not the 1960s anymore in Canada. Their cases illustrate that, in the case of a formal draft, fleeing to Canada may not be an option.

It is speculated that the current total number of deserters seeking asylum in Canada is less than a dozen. While these men have gained the ire of many of Canada's influential daily newspaper columnists, they have become a *cause celebre* in the anti-war movement there.

Americans seeking "refugee status" must go before the Immigration and Refugee Board, and must prove a claim of persecution based on religion, nationality, race, or membership in a specific social group or political opinion.

During the '60s, draft evaders could live in Canada while waiting for a hearing. Today, Canadian law requires that any asylum seeker wait in their home country while the application is processed.

Also, during the '60s, it was easier to make a case to stay in Canada as it had no draft. Yet military desertion is a crime in both Canada and the United States.

Interestingly enough, there are some fascinating Canadian legal precedents that may be in the American military deserters' favor. Soldiers from the armies of both Iraq and Iran have been granted refugee status in Canada. One, a Yemeni citizen serving in the Iraqi Army, had refused to participate in Saddam Hussein's invasion of Kuwait. The Iranian soldier had refused to be a party to chemical warfare. Significantly, both men were at first denied refugee status by the Immigration and Refugee Board, only to have the decisions reversed in federal court.

The Gay Claim

The confusing policy called "Don't Ask, Don't Tell" created in 1993 preserved the illegal status of homosexuals in the Armed Services. This policy says that as long as gay or bisexual men and women in the military hide anything that could let other people know that they are gay, commanders won't try to investigate their sexuality and kick them out of the service. Since a formal draft has not yet been reinstated, it is impossible to know exactly how the admission of "homosexual acts" would play out today. In the Vietnam era, as in previous wars, the military routinely barred gays and lesbians from military duty, and being gay was a way to avoid serving in the military when drafted.

In the late '60s, when anti-war sentiment was at an all-time high, there were plenty of gay men who were happy not to get an induction notice. Other men, such as a heterosexual named Tony Thompson, told the draft board he was gay in order to avoid conscription. "I just went in there and told them that I was gay. There was no way I was going to fight in that war. They believed me, and I got out."

San Francisco activist Tommi Avicolli-Mecca remembers a neighbor who outed himself in order to avoid being drafted. At the time, many gay people kept their gay identity a secret to avoid problems at work and in everyday life. Being gay was not accepted, nor even talked about, in the way it is today. In the 1960s, it was considered a form of mental illness. "There was a guy in my neighborhood who walked into the South Philly induction center around 1969 and convinced them he was gay. He was, but back then you had to convince the military of that fact. He wore a hint of makeup, carried a purse, etc. Classic routine at the time, but he pulled it off with grace and finesse. I loved that guy.

"Since I went to college in the fall of '69 and remained there until 1974 I never had to prove that I was morally opposed to war. I goofed around college and worked my butt off just to keep paying tuition. Fortunately I went to Temple University, Philly's state-funded school, that many working-class kids like myself attended to get an education. I spent a lot of my time organizing on campus for the Gay Liberation Front and against the war."

The National Guard

"I am angry that so many of the sons of the powerful and well-placed... managed to wangle slots in Reserve and National Guard units... Of the many tragedies of Vietnam, this raw class discrimination strikes me as the most damaging to the ideal that all Americans are created equal ..." — former Secretary of State Colin Powell

What is The National Guard? The National Guard was created in 1903 by the Dick Act, which reorganized state militias into National Guard units to assist states in times of local emergencies like floods, earthquakes, fires, and other disasters, and to protect the country as a whole in time of federal emergencies. Unlike regular Army soldiers who serve full time and are stationed on military bases, members of the Army National Guard serve only on weekends and live at home, except when they are called to active duty in time of emergency by their state's Governor or the President. This distinction allows members of the Guard to attend college and work full-time jobs.

During the Vietnam War Era Much discussion has occurred about President Bush's time in the National Guard during the Vietnam War. Underneath all of the talk lies a far more important tale: the National Guard during the 1960s was a place for sons of the wealthy to serve stateside and avoid combat in Vietnam. Former Vice-President Dan Quayle also spent time in the Guard. During the Vietnam War, the waiting list for the National Guard was usually long, as many young men sought to avoid combat. President Bush was sworn in the same day he applied, as his father (who would become Vice-President under Ronald Reagan in the 1980s and then President himself) was a congressman from Houston at the time. Many socially or politically prominent young men were admitted to the Texas Air National Guard, according to former officials, including the son of then-Senator John Tower and at least seven members of the Dallas Cowboys football team.

How It Is Now In late 2003, President Bush drafted the National Guard into U.S. Military full-time service when he sent more than 37,000 National Guard soldiers to Iraq to replace forces already on the ground. It was the largest mobilization of the National Guard since the Korean War. National Guard soldiers served in Vietnam, the Gulf War, and Kosovo, but only in a limited capacity and in the latter two wars without any fatalities. Since then, National Guard mobilizations have escalated with a new unit being called to active duty every few weeks. The use of National Guard soldiers in Iraq far exceeds its use compared to other wars. As of June 5, 2005, the National Guard accounted for 45% of the total Army force in Iraq. Since the beginning of the wars in Iraq and Afghanistan, 210,000 of the Guard's 330,000 soldiers have been called up to active duty, serving tours of duty that often last twenty months. More than two hundred Army National Guard soldiers have already died in Iraq, more than double the amount that died in the entire Vietnam War.

As it stands now, the National Guard is no longer a certain way to avoid active combat.

What Continues to Work

Going 4-F: Unfit to Serve

If you don't pass the physical or mental examination during induction, your status will be 4-F. You may have to serve, but will be declared unfit for the battlefield. During the Vietnam-era draft, James Fallows, a Harvard graduate and former editor for *U.S. News & World Report,* had this experience.

On the day of his pre-induction physical examination, Fallows and all of the other registrants from Harvard and Cambridge arrived at the Boston Army Base with letters from doctors and psychiatrists that would keep them from being drafted. In the weeks leading up to the physical, Fallows starved himself and dropped his weight to 120 pounds, making him virtually useless to the army. Meanwhile, as the Harvard graduates were being processed, a busload of healthy working-class young men arrived. Fallows quickly realized that they knew nothing about draft loopholes. On that day, the middle-class kids escaped the draft as the working-class boys went off to war.

Following are excerpts from the Army's "Standards of Medical Fitness", as of February 2004. Just a few of the causes for rejection (and there are many more) for enlistment and induction are:

Men: Height below 60 inches or over 80 inches.
Women: Height below 58 inches or over 80 inches.

Maximum Body Fat Percentages:

Female —	Age 17-20: 30%	Male —	Age 17-20: 24%
	21-27: 32%		21-27: 26%
	28-39: 34%		28-39: 28%
	40+: 36%		40+: 30%

Among the causes for rejection for enlistment and induction are a history of neurotic, anxiety, or mood disorders resulting in any or all of the below:

— Care by a physician or other mental health professional for more than six months.

— Symptoms or behavior of a repeated nature that impaired social, school, or work efficiency.

— Suicide, history of attempted or suicidal behavior.

Common conditions which would cause rejection for induction include asthma, any type of diabetes, and allergies including a history of anaphylaxis to stinging insects or moderate to severe reaction to common foods, spices, or food additives.

The Case of Chris Faiers: Leave the Country

In June of 1969, Chris Faiers received three draft notices in a week, and it was time to decide. Until then he had managed to appeal numerous draft notices for several years through his student deferment. Chris's situation was somewhat unique (as was everyone else's) in that he was a Canadian national by birth but was still eligible for the draft as a "resident alien".

When he received the three draft notices in a week, and the draft board (in Atlanta, Georgia, where Chris had lived just prior to moving to Miami, Florida) took away his student deferment, his parents suggested that Chris go live in England with his cousin. Faiers went to live with relatives in England and then settled in Canada, where he continues to reside.

The most popular destination countries for evading the draft during the Vietnam War were Canada, Mexico, Britain, and Sweden. Sweden granted Vietnam-era deserters humanitarian asylum based on "special circumstances."

In Good Conscience: An Interview with Conscientious Objector Aidan Delgado by Scott Fleming

Editor's Note: The following excerpt originally appeared in LiP magazine, Spring 2005. It is from an interview with Spc. Aidan Delgado, an enlisted soldier in the Army Reserve who spent a one-year tour of Iraq working to get his Conscientious Objector status approved. It was finally approved after he returned from active combat.

Aidan Delgado, 23, was a Florida college student looking for a change when he decided to join the Army Reserve. It was his misfortune to sign an enlistment contract on the morning of September 11, 2001. After finishing the paperwork, he saw a television broadcast of the burning World Trade Center and realized he might be in for more than one weekend a month of low-key service. In the ensuing months, Delgado became dedicated to Buddhism and its principles of pacifism. By April 2003, when he began his yearlong tour in Iraq, he was openly questioning whether he could participate in the war there in good conscience. Having grown up in Cairo, Egypt, Delgado spoke Arabic and had not been steeped in the racism that drove many of his fellow soldiers. When he surrendered his rifle and declared himself a Conscientious Objector in the middle of 2003, he was punished by his officers and ostracized by his peers. His unit, the 320th Military Police Company, spent six months in the southern city of Nasiriyah, and another six months helping to run the notorious Abu Ghraib prison outside Baghdad.

Why did you decide to join the Army?

It was not for high-minded reasons. I was in school, but I wasn't doing all that well. I was stagnating. I wanted to get a change of scenery, do something different. I signed up for the Reserves, because in the pre-September 11 world, the Reserves meant you work just two days a month; you get to be in the Army, but you don't have to do anything. I signed my contract the morning of September 11 and then all of a sudden my Reserve commitment meant a whole lot more.

How did you feel about your decision to join the Army in light of what happened that day?

At the time, the whole country was riding high on this surge of patriotism, so I felt vindicated, that I had made the right decision. Because I joined before September 11, I felt morally superior — I joined before it was popular to do so. Afterwards, when I saw the September 11 feelings being redirected — Afghanistan was one thing, but then they started turning it toward Iraq — my feelings of patriotism waned.

It wasn't long after 9/11, maybe six months, that the Bush administration started publicly building the case for invading Iraq.

Yeah, that's what I thought was very striking. I felt like they had made a very strong case for attacking the Taliban and the whole Afghanistan campaign. But when they started talking about Iraq, I said, "Wait, there isn't any proven connection, and there are several facts that seem to indicate they were not connected."

How did Buddhism influence your feelings about the army and the war in Iraq?

My Buddhism developed parallel to being in the Army. I wasn't a Buddhist before I joined the military, but after I signed on I had a couple of months before I went to basic training. That's when I started studying Buddhism intensely, doing research to cope with the stress of being in the Army.

I went into advanced training the next summer, and that's when I became really serious about Buddhism. I became a vegetarian. I started talking to my sergeants, saying, "I'm not sure the Army's right for me; I'm a Buddhist now."

Within a few months of arriving in Iraq, I told them that I wanted to be a Conscientious Objector and I wanted to leave the military because of my religious beliefs. It ended up taking over a year to get my CO status, so I served in the whole conflict as a Conscientious Objector. I finally got Conscientious Objector status after my unit returned to the U.S.

How hard was it to get Conscientious Objector status?

Extremely difficult — there's a huge burden of proof. You have to do an interview with an investigating officer who grills you on your beliefs to find out if you're just making it up or if you've really thought it out. You have to have some kind of documentation. I think one of my strongest points was that I had a lot of military paperwork showing that I had gradually identified myself as a Buddhist. I also had a lot of conversations with my superiors where I talked about being an Objector and being a Buddhist, and they went on the record and said, "Yes, he's talked about it progressively throughout the deployment." That really did a lot to establish my sincerity.

The command was extremely hostile to me, and there were all kinds of punitive measures. They wouldn't let me go on leave. They took my ballistic armor away — they told me that I didn't need the hard plate that goes inside your flak jacket, the part that actually protects you against bullets. They said that because I was an Objector and I wasn't going to fight, I wouldn't need it. This proved not to be the case; when we got to Abu Ghraib, there was continuous mortar shelling. I did the whole year's deployment without that plate. I really feel that was more maliciously motivated than anything else.

Also, I was socially ostracized. A lot of my fellow soldiers didn't want to eat with me or hang out with me or go on missions with me. They felt I was untrustworthy because I was critical of the war and I was a Buddhist. My command "lost" my Conscientious Objector paperwork or misdirected it. They'd say, "We lost your copy, you'll have to do it again."

I eventually got my home leave back because I threatened my commander that I was going to have them prosecuted for discriminating against me on religious grounds. My company commander, my company first sergeant, and my battalion commander had all decided they were not going to let me leave — they said I couldn't go home on a two-week leave because I wouldn't come back. I was going to get the ACLU and the World Congress of Buddhists involved. Ultimately, they decided it wasn't worth the headache.

Why did you decide to speak out about your experiences in Iraq?

At first, I just wanted to live quietly and leave the whole experience behind me. But then people started asking me about my war experiences. In a way, my first discussion was a response to all these people. I thought I would have a forum and talk to everybody at once and I would never have to tell anyone else ever again. As I went along, it snowballed and I gave a talk to my community—and that's when 400 people showed up.

After I spoke, people were really moved by what I had said. I received several offers to speak on college campuses in Florida. I don't think the American people are bad or willfully making wrong decisions. I think they're making misinformed decisions. If they had some more information, they wouldn't support the war and their views would change. That's really my goal, to create a sense of critical thinking, of disbelief, a sense of responsibility for the negative consequences of the war.

Have you made any links with other veterans who feel the way you do?

Yes. St. Pete for Peace is a group I've worked for, also Iraq Veterans Against the War, and Soldiers for Common Sense. My concern is that some of these groups haven't been very effective in creating a cogent movement. I feel that if I can personally draw 400 people with a slide show, there's no reason why a group like Iraq Veterans Against the War shouldn't be able to draw an audience of thousands. I look around America and am dismayed by how the war is on the back burner for people—it's not in their consciences. I want to make it something that's on the forefront of peoples' minds every day, rather than something you see occasionally on the news when something particularly bad happens.

What You Need To Know About Conscientious Objector Claims

"Today, I am in a position to make a difference or remain silent. Will I participate in a war which could lead to hundreds of thousands of civilian dead, endanger the safety of the American people and create chaos in the Middle East, all to benefit a few powerful and wealthy people?" — Ghanim Khalil, Army National Guard

There is a difference between becoming a CO and being a Resistor. A CO is someone who objects to all wars from a deeply held religious, moral, or ethical standpoint. A Resistor can be someone who does not fit that classification and therefore is not eligible for separation from the military or alternative service under the law.

Anyone faced with this choice should consult with a reliable enlistment counselor and weigh the consequences of each. Alan Solomonow of the American Friends Service Committee recommends going the CO route, "It is the most consistent position one could take and offers the most in the way of legal possibilities."

One soldier I spoke with, who asked to remain anonymous, remarked, "I disagree with the idea that becoming a CO is the only way to go. The military wants people to opt-out of war on their terms, so they can use you in another capacity, one that will still help them wage war. If I choose not to serve on moral grounds, then I'm out altogether."

Whatever the choice, it is important to make it with as much support from organizations, family and friends as possible.

Since the beginning of the invasion of Afghanistan, many dozens of enlisted people have applied for Conscientious Objector status. The ways in which these cases are being decided speak volumes for what military policy might look like should a formal draft be reinstated. Some, like former Marine Stephen Funk, have been successful, due in part to large scale public support. Others, such as Camilo Mejia and Jeremy Hinzman, have had their CO claims denied and either returned to the battlefield, fled the country, or served time in prison.

The Case of Marine Stephen Funk

Stephen Funk joined the Marine Corps in February of 2002 and went off to boot camp in May. He was nineteen at the time and felt like he was stuck in a cycle of bad decisions, and the military seemed like the perfect place to have decisions made for him. Previously, he had left the University of California for a three-month visit to the Philippines. When he returned, he found that his California residency had expired, so he entered a period of depression and aimlessness. "Military recruiters had been hounding me for months to join. I am not sure how they got my number, and I saw in the military what I felt was missing in my life: a sense of purpose and belonging."

Funk planned to train as a Military Support Specialist, but knew he was a CO while still in boot camp. "I seriously felt ill from having to stab human-shaped sandbags and be violent towards other recruits. I remember in a letter I wrote home saying that boot camp is the exact opposite of civilized training. You are praised for being violent and for stupidity. During boot camp I attributed my feelings to the stress. In my CO application, they ask for a crystallizing moment. I wrote about an experience I had on the rifle range during rifle qualifications. I shot well (expert class) but my instructor told me he thought I would not do that well in real combat. I was confused at first and bitter because I had done well and then I realized he was right. I told him that he was right that I would not do well because I don't believe it is right to kill people and would never shoot at someone. It was the first time in training that I vocally connected with my feelings about the training."

Funk doesn't believe that most enlisted people think about their feelings towards war until faced with one. He adds, "During my lifetime, the U.S. had only been in conflict during Gulf War I, which was when I was 12. The issue of war had never been brought up for me."

The process of applying for CO status is extremely trying. After completing the paper application, potential COs are "interviewed by a chaplain, a psychiatrist, and an investigative officer." The process is very drawn out and usually takes six months to a year. While Funk originally went Absent Without Leave (AWOL), he returned and explained to his command that he would not be showing up for Reservist drills until his application was complete. "I used the time to throw a press conference and create attention to the option of Conscientious Objection."

In contrast to some enlisted people who became CO, Funk was treated fairly well. Following the press conference, he was sent to active duty in New Orleans in April 2003. His hearing wasn't until September, so he was put to work setting up parades and events.

Funk believes that there are plenty more COs in the military but few know of the options. He advises activists to remember something he knows very personally. "Most importantly counter-recruitment activists need to highlight the choices young people have. Many enlist because they feel like it is their only option."

He also urges anti-war folks to stay pro-active. "The counter-recruiters need to get to people before the recruiters do and get them the information that recruiters don't want them to know. Honestly, there are benefits for joining the military but these benefits can be gained elsewhere. We need to get it into people's heads that the price paid for military benefits is way too high."

Becoming a Conscientious Objector

"If you were given an order to participate in an unlawful occupation that is resulting in the deaths of thousands of innocent people with no justifiable cause, would you be able to live with yourself if you carried out that order?" — Brandon Hughey, U.S. Army 1st Cavalry now seeking asylum in Canada

What follows is a step-by step guide to building a Conscientious Objector (CO) case, whether you are already in the military, or a civilian preparing for the possibility of a formal draft. Seek detailed advice from an experienced Recruitment Counselor before taking action. In wartime, laws and regulations can change quickly so don't rely on any single book, pamphlet, video, or speech to base your decisions and strategy upon.

This information is based on federal regulations, documents, and some extremely useful publications published by counter-recruitment organizations. For a complete list of sources for further reading, please consult the bibliography in the back of this book.

Remember, becoming a CO is not the only way that enlisted and drafted people choose to resist war. The military is making it more difficult for people to qualify for CO status. Many choose not to participate in the process altogether, pointing out that those who seek "alternative enlistment" can aid the war efforts without ever firing a shot. In times of war, many others choose to rebel and organize from inside the military.

There is simply no one "right way" to resist, just tactics and strategies that are shaped not only by one's beliefs, but social movements and historical moments. No matter what an individual's choice may be, each is taking an immense risk to refuse orders in any shape or form while handing warmakers a real crisis: refusal to go to war.

Frequently Asked Questions:
Establishing CO Status Before a Draft Happens

What is a Conscientious Objector?

A CO is a person who rejects all war, for any reason. Technically, this leaves out a large portion of the population, since many people sanction some kind of war under certain circumstances. Legally, one can still support the use of violence for personal self-defense and still qualify for CO status. While it is not necessary to believe in God, you do have to demonstrate that your anti-war values are rooted in a religious, moral or ethical belief system.

A CO is exempt from military combat service but in the event of a draft may be required to perform "alternative" service to the federal government in some way.

Who is required to register for the draft?

Men between the ages of eighteen and twenty-five must register with the Selective Service System within thirty (30) days of their eighteenth (18th) birthday. Some activists advocate massive refusal to register in order to make it difficult for the SSS to prepare a draft.

The last time anyone was prosecuted for not registering with the Selective Service System was 1985. While this may seem like an easy way to protest war, one should do so knowing the possible consequences. It is well known that the many people join the military to get money for college; and the military has also cleverly worked to cut off college possibilities for those who do not register. In some states, state financial aid is denied to non-registrants, and federal student aid is out of the question to these people as well. Likewise, many states bar non-registrants from government employment, and federal jobs are strictly off limits. Non-citizens (resident aliens) who choose not to register are also barred from U.S. citizenship.

All that over a postcard? It gets worse. Many states are now considering legislation that would withhold diplomas and driver's licenses to those who refuse to register.

If I'm a CO, do I have to register? Is there anything I can do to prepare my CO case when I register? How do I prove it?

Yes. COs are encouraged to write 'I am a Conscientious Objector opposed to participating in a war of any form' on their registration cards. Photocopy the card, and mail a copy to yourself because Selective Service destroys the original registration cards after they are processed.

Prepare a personal statement of your beliefs, and how you developed them. It is good to be able to demonstrate how these values influence your daily life. Keep a record of anti-war organizations you belong to, books that deepened your anti-war stance. Letters of support are crucial and back up the point that your beliefs are deeply held, not recently acquired.

What about young women?

As of this writing, women are not required by law to register with the Selective Service. The last proposed draft, the defeated Rangel Bill, conscripted women as well as men. It is assumed that at some point the SSS will be reformed to include women as well.

Documenting Your CO Status: Their Questions

If you decide to declare CO status, you will have to answer seven questions if you are already in the Army, and six if you are in any other branch of the military. In the event of a formal draft, it is likely that most of these questions will still apply, providing that CO status is still allowed at that time.

How have your beliefs developed? When did you know you were a CO? How is your life different now?

If already in the military, ask yourself what your beliefs were when you enlisted and how and when they evolved.

Your essay should be able to trace the evolution of your thoughts on war. Did you have significant life-changing events that made your beliefs clear? Did you read a book, see a movie? Did basic training burst some illusions you had about the righteousness of war?

Most importantly, how do you live your life differently as a result of this change?

What is the nature of your beliefs?

One of the biggest myths about CO declarations is that your claim must be based on your religious beliefs. Of course, religious objections to war are some of the easiest to document especially if you belong to a church, like the Quakers, with a tradition of opposing war. Yet those whose beliefs stem from moral or ethical standpoints may also gain CO status,

Do you believe that the use of force is ever defensible?

This question is easy to get tripped up on. Remember, the

law clearly states that you must have a deeply felt objection to war — not every single use of force. You can still be a CO even if you would defend your mother if she was mugged in front of you, or even if you would defend yourself if assaulted in a bar. While some might believe that all violence is wrong, the law still recognizes that there is a massive difference between armed conflict and a fist fight.

The trick question: How deeply held is the belief?

To gain CO status, one must object to wars that one could reasonably be asked to fight in one's lifetime. It is irrelevant whether or not you would have fought Hitler, what you would do if Attila the Hun's armies came knocking on your door, how you would have felt if you grew up under South African apartheid, lived during the time of the Civil War and so on.

However, COs should be prepared to answer questions about whether they would take up arms against a dictatorship in the U.S., or if you think there could be times when revolutionary violence is necessary.

The Case of Jerry Chernow

In 1970, Jerry Chernow became a draft resister when his application for CO status was denied. "I applied for CO status and was turned down," Chernow said. "It was very difficult to get CO status at the time."

Chernow appealed to the state board and was denied CO status again. When he received his induction notice in the mail, he ignored it until a draft counselor advised him to get a lawyer. His lawyer suggested asking for another induction date and then refusing to serve again at that time. Chernow did so and was arrested in January 1971. The FBI interrogated him and stuck him in a federal prison. He was released on a signature bond until his trial nearly seven months later. The charges against him were dropped.

The possibility of jail time didn't stop Chernow from sticking to his beliefs, but he encourages young people to be better prepared than he was, in hopes that they can avoid the threat of prison.

"I would suggest not just thinking about military issues, but to start writing their thoughts down," Chernow said. "Document everything — whether it is an anti-war rally you've attended or books you've read — and save all that."

Getting Out Once You Are In

If you are already in the military, documenting a CO claim is nearly identical to the one that civilians would use in the case of an actual formal draft. For those in the Army wanting to get out, the choice is Discharge or Separation. If you are classified 'separated' from the military, the government still has you on a rope and can pull you back out of inactivity or reserve status. Separation can result in transfer to alternative service or the Individual Ready Reserves. Many people choose to serve out the remainder of an enlistment in this manner, however only the classification of 'discharge' guarantees that you will not be called up to serve again.

What follows is only a primer: call the GI Rights Hotline (1-800-394-9544) prior to taking any action towards leaving the military.

Wait a minute, the recruiter promised me computer training but I'm on latrine duty!

There are volumes of regulations that provide for discharge or separation because of "erroneous, defective or fraudulent enlistment." You must file the complaint within thirty (30) days of discovering that you would not receive whatever was promised to you to secure your enlistment.

According to the GI Rights Hotline, "You must show that your enlistment would have never occurred if the facts had been known or if recruiting personnel had followed regulations." This can take many forms, and it is best to consult with a Draft Counselor in order to document your claim of "erroneous, defective, or fraudulent" enlistment.

Also, if you were promised training by your recruiter that you did not and will not receive, you may be eligible for separation or discharge.

Can I be a Conscientious Objector even though I'm already in the military?

Yes. You can apply for CO status, although be prepared to answer hard questions about why you enrolled in the military in the first place. The military recognizes two kinds of conscientious objectors. "Class 1-0" objectors are against any kind of participation in the military, and are seeking to leave altogether. A "Class 1-A-O" is willing to stay in the military as a noncombatant. Remember being declared a noncombatant won't keep you from a combat zone. Ethically speaking, many people consider noncombatant classification as still participating in war, as the military needs clerical workers and medics in order to carry one out. You should be clear on your position before making a CO claim.

What about Don't Ask, Don't Tell? Can I get out if I'm gay?

Today, many military personnel, gay and straight might be tempted to make the Gay Claim in order to be excused from service. It is not as simple as putting on a dress or French kissing a member of the same sex.

Although one can be discharged for a homosexual act or if one states he or she is homosexual, such admissions can result in a Dishonorable Discharge. The Central Committee for Conscientious Objectors urges gays who wish to be discharged honorably to seek the advice of an attorney. Those considering this path must remember: don't admit to "acts," don't name names, and don't under any circumstances, admit to a history of gay conduct.

Any admission of such conduct will lead to an investigation of your private life, and that intrusion can include urinalysis — as many in the military brass still equate the gay lifestyle with drug abuse.

What if I'm my parent's only son or daughter?
Contrary to widespread belief, being an only son or daughter will not get you out of the military. However, if you are enlisted and your father, mother, brother or sister is killed while serving in the U.S. military, you may be discharged or separated from the military.

Counter-Recruitment and Active Dissent Create A Storm

As of this writing, more voices of dissent are emerging. Over four dozen soldiers have applied for Conscientious Objector (CO) status, and many others have gone AWOL. In addition, a counter-recruitment movement has confronted military recruiters on campuses and communities nationwide. These high-profile actions have sprung up in both liberal and conservative areas, a strong counterpoint to the notion that Bush was handed a mandate for unlimited war. For example:

Madison, Wisconsin: Five protesters are arrested after refusing to leave a military recruiting station until it was turned into a financial aid office.

Boston, Massachusetts: A Boston College student was charged with making a false bomb threat after standing on a milk crate outside a recruiting station wearing a black hood and cape with attached stereo wires to his hands to protest torture at Abu Ghraib prison.

Philadelphia, Pennsylvania: Demonstrating against the Bush Administration's cuts to homeless services members of Kensington Welfare Rights Union barricade a local recruiting office.

Seattle, Washington: Following a high school walk-out involving several hundred students, military recruiters are chased from campus by youth.

Mayaguez, Puerto Rico: Under the leadership of Frente Universitario por la Desmilitarización y la Educación (FUDE), activists have used civil disobedience to directly block the construction of a new Air Force recruiting station.

New York, New York: At a college job fair, three students

were arrested after they stood up in front of a National Guard recruitment table chanting anti-war slogans.

Wayne, New Jersey: A student at William Patterson University is charged with "defiant trespassing" while passing out anti-recruitment fliers near a military recruitment table.

South Carolina: Thirteen members of the 1st Battalion of the 178th Field Artillery Regiment of the South Carolina Army National Guard go absent without leave (AWOL) during training exercises. The remaining 635 soldiers of the unit are confined to their barracks for two weeks before being shipped out to Iraq.

San Diego, California: Petty Officer 3rd Class Pablo Paredes of the Bronx refuses to board a ship taking 3,000 Marines to Iraq. "I don't want to be a part of a ship that's taking 3,000 Marines over there, knowing a hundred or more of them won't come back," he said. "I can't sleep at night knowing that's what I do for a living."

Supporting Soldiers Who Question Orders

When a soldier decides to resist war they put everything — life, safety, friendship and financial security — at risk. Whether they become a resistor or a CO means very little to their commanders, who are likely to treat any form of disobedience with contempt. Likewise they are probably receiving mixed messages from home, political groups and the press over the righteousness of their actions.

Aimee Allison remembers her own journey that took her from the military to a CO declaration and into anti-war activism.

"In the history of the anti-war movement, there has traditionally been angst around supporting soldiers, whether or not they resist. I didn't start questioning war until I was in an environment, college, where questions about everything were being asked. Today, the most powerful anti-war voices are soldiers. I tell soldiers that duty, service and responsibility are all good paths but there are many ways to live out those values.

Military recruiters take a very family-oriented approach to bringing people into the military. The best counter-recruiters do, as well.

"We try to work with the moms and dads, the family members of military people who choose to resist. Chances are that there was turmoil when the family member went into the military and there will be turmoil if they want to leave. We want to make the soldier feel like they have some support," remarked Allison.

Individuals with friends or family members who resist can make life easier by not being judgmental of the choice, not talking to military authorities, and generally being a good friend: returning phone calls, helping to find legal support, checking in on the enlisted person's loved ones if appropriate.

Anti-war groups should go slow with objectors, building and honoring trust between the organization and the individual. This means not pushing the soldier into speaking at rallies unless he or she wants to and understands the possible consequences. A group wishing to work with soldiers should know that if they put the needs and safety of the soldier first, they will likely develop a rapport and a possible lifelong supporter. This isn't to say that soldiers who object should not speak at rallies. On the contrary, any chance at turning public opinion against war depends on dissent from within the ranks. If a CO has a case pending against him or her, at least consult with a lawyer before putting a microphone in front of them.

Allison explains, "We need to embrace questioning soldiers both personally and organizationally. You are asking someone to overcome intense training and conditioning. A potential resistor is at risk in so many ways. It is important to put their needs in the forefront. It is now impossible to be declared a CO if one has disobeyed orders, so organizations that work with enlisted people who are considering resisting or declaring themselves a CO have to be careful when asking soldiers to appear at anti-war events. You have to work with the families and friends, call often and check in."

Likewise, in the event of a formal draft, seek out the support of an experienced draft counselor and anti-war organization. Connect with the organized anti-war community — there is safety and strength in numbers — don't go it alone!

**UNITED STATES DEPARTMENT OF EDUCATION
UNITED STATES DEPARTMENT OF DEFENSE**

October 9, 2002

Dear Colleague

For more than 25 years, the Armed Forces of our Nation have been staffed entirely by volunteers. The All-Volunteer Force has come to represent American resolve to defend freedom and protect liberty around the world. Sustaining that heritage requires the active support of public institutions in presenting military opportunities to our young people for their consideration.

Recognizing the challenges faced by military recruiters, Congress recently passed legislation that requires high schools to provide to military recruiters, upon request, access to secondary school students and directory information on those students. Both the *No Child Left Behind Act of 2001* and the *National Defense Authorization Act for Fiscal Year 2002* reflect these requirements.

In accordance with those Acts, military recruiters are entitled to receive the name, address, and telephone listing of juniors and seniors in high school. As clarified in the enclosure, providing this information is consistent with the *Family Educational Rights and Privacy Act*, which protects the privacy of student education records. Student directory information will be used specifically for armed services recruiting purposes and for informing young people of scholarship opportunities. For some of our students, this may be the best opportunity they have to get a college education.

The support by our Nation's educational institutions on behalf of the U.S. Armed Forces is critical to the success of the All-Volunteer Force. It can be, and should be, a partnership that benefits everyone. As veterans, and as Cabinet Members serving the President, we can attest to the excellent educational opportunities the military affords, as well as an environment that encourages the development of strong character and leadership skills.

The Department of Education and Department of Defense have worked together to provide you the enclosed guidelines for compliance with these new laws. We encourage you to examine the enclosed information carefully and to work closely with military recruiters as they carry out their important public responsibilities.

Sincerely,

Rod Paige
Secretary of Education

Donald H. Rumsfeld
Secretary of Defense

Enclosure

Propaganda letter sent to high school administrators by Departments of Defense and Education in support of the No Child Left Behind Act

No Child Left Unrecruited

"The reason to have a military is to be prepared to fight and win wars. The military is not a social-welfare agency. It is not a jobs program." — Vice-President Dick Cheney

"If the purpose of the GI Bill is to get veterans into school, it is not accomplishing the task. ... [GI Bill] benefits cover a fraction of the cost of a contemporary education at an average four-year college."
— Congressional Commission on Servicemembers and Veterans Transition Assistance, 1999

The "No Child Left Behind Act" passed into law in 2001 received heavy criticism from educators across the political spectrum for its requirement that schools introduce rigid standardized testing in order to receive federal funds. At the time, few noticed the section which forces schools to "share" student information with military recruiters.

SEC. 9528. ARMED FORCES RECRUITER ACCESS TO STUDENTS AND STUDENT RECRUITING INFORMATION.
(a) POLICY-
(1) ACCESS TO STUDENT RECRUITING INFORMA-TION- Notwithstanding section 444(a)(5)(B) of the General Education Provisions Act and except as provided in paragraph (2), each local educational agency receiving assistance under this Act shall provide, on a request made by military recruiters or an institution of higher education, access to secondary school students names, addresses, and telephone listings.

(2) CONSENT- A secondary school student or the parent of the student may request that the student's name, address, and telephone listing described in paragraph (1) not be released without prior written parental consent, and the local educational agency or private school shall notify parents of the option to make a request and shall comply with any request.

(3) SAME ACCESS TO STUDENTS- Each local educational agency receiving assistance under this Act shall provide military recruiters the same access to secondary school students as is provided generally to post secondary educational institutions or to prospective employers of those students.

(b) NOTIFICATION- The Secretary, in consultation with the Secretary of Defense, shall, not later than 120 days after the date of enactment of the No Child Left Behind Act of 2001, notify principals, school administrators, and other educators about the requirements of this section.

(c) EXCEPTION- The requirements of this section do not apply to a private secondary school that maintains a religious objection to service in the Armed Forces if the objection is verifiable through the corporate or other organizational documents or materials of that school.

However, there is a simple way to prevent military recruiters from obtaining information about students. When the school knows about and lets families know about, there is an "opt out" provision. Either the parent or guardian, or student (if age 18), can explicitly provide in writing that the student's personal information cannot be released without prior written consent.

The Myth of the Progressive Draft

Just over thirty years after the end of the Vietnam War, some legislators who wish to bring back a draft come armed with the language of social justice: why should only the poor fight?

These voices are absolutely correct: poor people do indeed bear the brunt of the fighting and dying in the War on Terror. Yet the argument ignores the simple fact that the way to pursue social justice is to work for it, joining the efforts for living wages, effective education, against discrimination, and so on. Programs like the ones sponsored by the Corporation for National Service (www.nationalservice.org/800-942-2677) including Americorps, VISTA, and the National Civilian Community Corps hire 40,000 people a year to do service work while earning money for college. There are peaceful alternatives.

Providing even more bodies to a war machine in search of cannon fodder will produce neither equity nor peace — save the possible sad equity and peace of graveyards.

APPENDIX A

Draft Induction Statistics:

Draft inductions by year from World War I through the end of the draft (7/1/73)

Year Inductions

1917:   516,212

1918: 2,294,084

1940:   18,633

1941:   923,842

1942: 3,033,361

1943: 3,323,970

1944: 1,591,942

1945:   945,862

1946:   183,383

1948:   20,348

1949:   9,781

1950:   219,771

1951:   551,806

1952:   438,479

1953:   471,806

1954:   253,230

1955:   152,777

1956:   137,940

1957:   138,504

1958:   142,246

1959:   96,153

1960:   86,602

1961:   118,586

1962:	82,060
1963:	119,265
1964:	112,386
1965:	230,991
1966:	382,010
1967:	228,263
1968:	296,406
1969:	283,586
1970:	162,746
1971:	94,092
1972:	49,514
1973:	646

The draft ended on July 1, 1973

[Source: Selective Service System]

APPENDIX B

Draft Board Classifications

Based on Vietnam-era information. The following is a list of Selective Service classifications that could be assigned by draft boards:

Classification / Definition

I-A Available for military service

I-A-0 Conscientious objector available for noncombatant military service only

I-C Member of the armed forces of the U.S., the Coast and Geodetic Survey, or the Public Health Service

I-D Member of reserve component or student taking military training

I-H Registrant not currently subject to processing for induction

I-0 Conscientious objector available for civilian work contributing to the maintenance of the national health, safety, or interest

I-S Student deferred by statute (High School)

I-Y Registrant available for military service, but qualified for military only in the event of war or national emergency

I-W Conscientious objector performing civilian work contributing to the maintenance of the national health, safety, or interest

II-A Registrant deferred because of civilian occupation (except agriculture or activity in study)

II-C Registrant deferred because of agricultural occupation

II-D Registrant deferred because of study preparing for the ministry

II-S Registrant deferred because of activity in study

III-A Registrant with a child or children; registrant deferred by reason of extreme hardship to dependents

IV-A Registrant who has completed service; sole surviving son

IV-B Official deferred by law

IV-C Alien

IV-D Minister of religion or divinity student

IV-F Registrant not qualified for any military service

IV-G Registrant exempt from service during peace (surviving son or brother)

IV-W Conscientious objector who has completed alternate service contributing to the maintenance of the national health, safety, or interest in lieu of induction into the Armed Forces of the United States

V-A Registrant over the age of liability for military service

Appendix C

The Military Recruitment Index

Total number of soldiers enlisted in all branches of the U.S. Military: 1,387,474[1]

Total number of soldiers deployed overseas: 206,410

Approximate number of soldiers serving in Iraq: 140,000[2]

Countries which President George W. Bush has mentioned he would consider invading: North Korea, Iran, Afghanistan, and Iraq

Total decrease of soldiers from all branches of the U.S. Military since George Bush was reelected: 30,780[3]

Annual amount the U.S. Military spends on recruiting: 2.6 million

Annual number of soldiers the influential conservative think tank Project For A New American Century urged Congress to add to the Army and Marine Corps: 25,000

Approximate number of National Guard reservists who have been deployed in Iraq and Afghanistan: 364,000

Average tour of duty for reservists: 20 months [4]

Percent drop in ROTC recruitment 2003-2005: 16%[5]

Percent drop in Army Recruitment February 2005: 27%

Percent of African-Americans in the U.S. Army: 23%

Percent of African-Americans in total population: 14.7%

Percent by which the U.S. Army missed its recruitment goals in April 2005: 42%[6]

Total number of "stop-loss" orders issued since the beginning of the War On Terror:11[7]

Minimum amount of Iraqi civilian deaths as of July 2005: 22, 787

Maximum amount of Iraqi civilian deaths as of July 2005: 25,814[8]

Total number of U.S. soldiers dead as of October 2005: 2,000[9]

-----

[1] U.S. Department of Defense
[2] Boston Globe
[3] December 2004-May 2004
[4] www.iraqometer.com
[5] Mens News Daily
[6] *Newsweek*
[7] www.optruth.org
[8] Iraq Body Count:www.iraqbodycount.net
[9] Antiwar.com

National & Regional

Most of these national organizations have branches across the United States, call to find one near you.

American Friends Service Committee Pacific Mountain Region
65 9th Street
San Francisco, CA 94103
(415) 565-0201

American Friends Service Committee
Youth & Militarism Program
1502 Cherry Street
Philadelphia, PA 19102
(215) 241-7176
www.youth4peace.org

The American Friends Service Committee was founded in 1917 to provide young Quakers and other conscientious objectors an opportunity to serve those in need instead of fighting during World War I. Today, they continue to provide enlistment counseling and campaigns to keep recruiters off of campus,

Central Committee For Conscientious Objectors
1515 Cherry Street
Philadelphia, PA 19102

Central Committee for Conscientious Objectors
405 14th Street, Suite 3205
Oakland, CA 94612

Since 1948, The Central Committee for Conscientious Objectors has organized and supported individual and collective resistance to war and preparations for war. They are the sponsoring organization for *AWOL* magazine and were the first of the traditional CO groups to open their resources to young anti-war activists using hip-hop and youth culture.

Citizen Soldier
267 Fifth Ave., Suite 901
New York, NY 10016
(212) 679-2250
www.citizensoldier.net

Provides legal and political support to soldiers who refuse illegal or immoral orders. Has an extensive and impressive collection of books on militarism available for purchase on the website.

Not In Our Name
P.O. Box 20221
Greeley Square Station
New York, NY 10001-0006
(800) 956-6927
info@notinourname.net
www.notinourname.net

"We believe that as people living in the United States it is our responsibility to resist the injustices done by our government, in our names."

Pax Christi USA
532 West Eighth Street
Erie, PA 16502
(814) 453-4955
info@paxchristiusa.org
www.paxchristiusa.org

Provides solid information on becoming a CO; written with the Catholic community in mind.

Student Peace Action Network
1100 Wayne Ave., Suite 1020
Silver Springs, MD 20910
(301) 565-4050, ext. 324
SPAN@peace-action.org
www.studentpeaceaction.org

"SPAN is a grassroots peace and justice organization working from campuses across the United States. We organize for an end to physical, social, and economic violence caused by militarism at home and abroad. We campaign for nuclear abolition, disarmament, and an end to weapons trafficking. We support a foreign policy based on human rights and international cooperation, and a domestic agenda that supports human and environmental concerns, not Pentagon excess. War is not inevitable. We push for practical alternatives."

United for Peace and Justice
PO Box 607
Times Square Station
NY, NY 10108
(212) 868-5545
www.unitedforpeace.org

United for Peace and Justice is a coalition of more than 1300 local and national groups throughout the United States who have joined together to oppose our government's policy of permanent warfare and empire-building.

Veterans For Peace
216 South Meramec Ave
St. Louis, MO 63105
(314) 725-6005
www.veteransforpeace.org

Veterans For Peace is a national organization founded in 1985. It is structured around a national office in Saint Louis, MO and comprised of members across the country organized in chapters or as at-large members. The organization includes men and women veterans from World War II, Korea, Vietnam, the Gulf War, other conflicts and peacetime veterans. Veterans For Peace is an official Non-Governmental Organization (NGO) represented at the UN.

War Resisters League
339 Lafayette Street
New York, NY 10012
(800) 976-9699

One of the oldest anti-war organizations and a great source for information. Deeply steeped in the pacifist tradition, the WRL's Anti-Militarism Program focuses on the many devastating consequences of war and weaponry. Its youth program, ROOTS (Revolution Out of Truth and Struggle), focuses on counter-recruitment and the impact of militarism on targeted populations like youth of color and the poor. And the War Tax Resistance program supports those who refuse to pay for war.

A major part of WRL's program is to help people organize in their own communities where real change begins. WRL has a network of local groups and contacts around the country. The National Office sends out regular mailings to a key list of local organizers and has offered a training program for organizers. Other special materials include the *Organizers Manual*, the book *War Tax Resistance*, a terrific collection of buttons and posters, organizers' packets, and videos for parents and students on war toys and military recruiting.

California

Resource Center For Nonviolence
515 Broadway
Santa Cruz CA 95060
(831) 423-1626
information@rcnv.org
www.rcnv.org

The Resource Center for Nonviolence offers a wide-range of educational programs in the history, theory, methodology, and current practice of nonviolence as a force for personal and social change. Founded in 1976, the Resource Center has developed a variety of formats to explore the meaning of nonviolence and its prospects in shaping our daily lives and our work for social change.

Guerrero Azteca
PO Box 300221
Escondido, CA
www.guerreroazteca.org

Founded by Fernando Suarez del Sola, who lost a son in the Iraq war, this organization focuses primarily on recruitment education within the Latino community.

Committee Opposed to Militarism and the Draft
PO Box 13195
San Diego, CA 93175

"COMD is an anti-militarism organization that also challenges the institution of the military, its effect on society, its budget, its role abroad and at home, and the racism, sexism and homophobia that are inherent in the armed forces and Selective Service System. COMD activities include community education, direct action and youth outreach. Individuals sharing our goals are invited to become COMD activists and supporters."

United Teachers of Los Angeles Human Rights Committee
3303 Wilshire Blvd 10th Floor
Los Angeles, CA 90010
(213) 487-5561

A committee within the Teacher's Union of the Los Angeles Unified School District.

Colorado

Ft. Collins Peace and Justice
Strength Through Peace Committee
Fort Collins, CO
strengththroughpeace@yahoo.com

"Strength Through Peace, a project of CJPE (Center for Justice, Peace, and Environment), is a community of concerned people in Northern Colorado with a shared belief that social, political, and economic justice are essentials of peace and are the best defense against terrorism and war.

"We further believe that adherence to international law is of supreme importance when nations are confronted by violence form without. Our purpose is to influence the basic character and policies of the United States to pursue these ideals through popular education, advocacy, and direct action."

Indiana

Catholic Peace Fellowship
PO Box 4232
South Bend, IN 46634

The Catholic Peace Fellowship is an organization dedicated to practicing the Peace of Christ through ministry and education. CPF offers support to soldiers and veterans who are struggling with the contradiction between their own participation in war and their conscience. CPF also educates the Church community about the two options by which a Catholic may address conflict: Active Pacifism and Just War.

Specifically, CPF takes calls from members of the military through the GI Rights Hotline, publishes *The Sign of Peace* quarterly journal, holds workshops on War, Peace, and Conscience, and provides educational resources to the community. We pay heed to Dorothy Day's call to all Catholics to "urge a mighty league of Conscientious Objectors."

Kentucky

Students United For Peace and Justice
PO Box 21362
Louisville, KY 40221
(502) 821-8894

Broad-based student group that brings together counter-recruitment and economic justice issues.

New Jersey

Coalition for Peace Action
40 Witherspoon St.
Princeton NJ 08542
(609) 924-3052
www.peacecoalition.org

"We work to eliminate militarism through peace activism and peace education. We are an action peace based non-profit organization."

New York

New York Collective of Radical Educators
www.nycore.org
nycore2003@yahoo.com

"NYCRE has created a curriculum, 'Military Myths: Combating Military Recruitment in the Classroom' as part of a widespread response to the increased efforts of military recruiters in New York City high schools. Military Myths is a 5 day classroom curriculum created by teachers for teachers. We believe that drastic cuts in state and city education budgets are indicative of the war being waged against low-income youth, especially youth of color. We as teachers must proactively address military myths with our students and challenge them to seek alternatives to enlisting in the military."

Ohio

Survivors Take Action Against Abuse by Military Personnel, Inc.
500 Greene Tree Place
Fairborn, Ohio 4532
(937) 879-2568
www.staaamp.org

Primarily a support for women soldiers who have been sexu-
ally assaulted in the service; also active in the national
counter-recruitment efforts.

Oregon

Peace House
PO Box 524
Ashland, OR 97520
(541) 482.9625
info@peacehouse.net
www.peacehouse.net

Produces the training "Countering Military Recruitment in
our Public Schools: a training for students, parents, school staff
and community members."

Eugene Peaceworks
Committee for Countering Military Recruitment
454 Willamette St.
Eugene, OR 97401
(541) 343-8548

eugpeace@efn.org
www.eugenepeaceworks.org

Maintains a committee for countering military recruitment, and an excellent newsletter.

Pennsylvania

Leigh-Pocono Committee of Concern
313 W 4th Street
Bethlehem, PA 18015
(610) 691-8730
lepoco@postmark.net
www.lepoco.org

Active in public education efforts on war and militarism.

Youth Philadelphia Area War Resistance
youthpawr@riseup.net
lists.riseup.net/www/info/youthpawr

"Youth Philadelphia Area War Resistance (Youth PAWR) is a coalition of progressive high school and college student organizations in the Philadelphia area."

Puerto Rico

Proyecto Caribeno de Justicia y Paz
1424 Vieques
Puerto Rico 00765

(787) 741-0716
bieke@prorescatevieques.org
www.prorescatevieques.org

Active in the campaign against the military bombing of Vieques and counter-recruitment campaigns within Puerto Rico.

Texas

Non-Military Options for Youth
P.O. Box 49594
Austin, TX 78765
(512) 452-7140
jeffweb@bga.com
www.progresssiveaustin.org

"Non-Military Options for Youth offers information to youth about the choices they face upon leaving high school. We seek to balance the military recruitment campaign with a contrasting view on military enlistment and JROTC, to educate youth about nonmilitary alternatives for job training, finding jobs and college financial aid.

"We are available for classroom and group presentations, high school career fairs, and individual counseling. A special emphasis is placed on reaching youth of color and low-income youths who are disproportionately recruited into the military. Our resources include a growing group of committed volunteers, as well as a variety of literature, videos, and computer software."

Vermont

Brattleboro Area Peace and Justice
PO Box 911
Brattleboro, VT
www.brattleboropeaceandjustice.org

"BAPJG works with people and communities to initiate and support local and global peacemaking. We seek alternatives to war, terrorism and all forms of violence and oppression through education, discussion, creative expression and non-violent action."

Washington

Teen Peace Project
Port Townsend, WA
liz@teenpeace.org
www.teenpeace.org

A good comprehensive website put together by an activist mother.

Wisconsin

Madison Area Peace Coalition
29 N. Hancock #4
(608) 442-0030
Madison, WI
www.madpeace.org

Works with students, parents, teachers, veterans, the school board and others to curtail military recruiting in the schools.

Peace Action Wisconsin
1001 E. Keefe Ave.
Milwaukee, WI 53212
(414) 964-5158
www.PeaceActionWI.org

A peace and justice organization which works for a world where human needs are met, the environment is preserved, and the threats of war and nuclear weapons have been abolished.

Bibliography

Articles:

CNN.com, no author credited, "Rangel introduces bill to reinstate draft Rumsfeld says he sees no need for military draft" January 8th, 2003.

Cave, Damien "For Recruiters a Hard Toll From A Hard Sell" *New York Times* March 21, 2005.

Dobie, Kathy "AWOL in America: When Desertion is the Only Option" *Harper's* magazine, March 2005.

Keating, Kevin "Harass The Brass! Mutiny, Fragging and Desertions in the U.S. Military" [The Bad Days Will End. 1990]

Mitchell, Russ "Back Door Draft Raises Questions" (CBSNEWS.com, June 27, 2004)

Reuters News Service "U.S. Army Struggles For Recruits Amid Iraq War," Sunday March 6, 2005.

Scouras, Susan "Old Man's Draft for World War II", *West*

Virginia Archives and History News, Vol. V, No. 5, July 2004

Sevunts, Levon "U.S. Deserters' Bid For Asylum has Canada Abuzz," *The Washington Times*, December 23, 2004

Squitieri, Tom "Army expanding 'stop loss' order to keep soldiers from leaving" *USA Today* January 6, 2004

Moniz, D and Squitteri T. "Experts seek roots of military's racial makeup; Analysts look at economic and class factors" *USA Today* January 21, 2003.

Michael E. O'Hanlon, "Nobody Wants a Draft, but What if We Need One?" *Los Angeles Times*, October 13, 2004

Books:

Dunbar-Ortiz, Roxanne *"Red Dirt: Growing Up Okie"* (Verso, 1997)

Foley, Michael S., *"The War Machine: Draft Resistance During the Vietnam War"* (University of North Carolina, 2003)

GI Rights Hotline "Getting Out: A Guide to Military Discharges" (Central Committee For Conscientious Objectors)

Keith, Jeanette *"Rich Man's War, Poor Man's Fight: Race Class and Power in the Rural South During the First World War"* (University of North Carolina, 2004)

Lynd, Staughton "We Won't Go: Narratives of Resistance to World War II, the Korean War, the Vietnam War and the 1990-91 U.S.- Iraq War, and the 2003-U.S.-Iraq War" (Historians Against the War Pamphlet #2).

Macelear, Michael *"The Ten Thousand Day War: Vietnam 1945-1975"* (St. Martin's Press)

Powell, Colin *"My American Journey"* (Ballantine, 1996)

Salisbury, Harrison, ed. "Vietnam: Lessons From A War"

Tracy, James (no relation to editor) *"Direct Action: Radical*

Pacifism From the Union Eight to the Chicago Seven" (University of Chicago Press, 1996).

Zinn, Howard. *A People's History of the United States*. (1980, Harper)

Whiteclay, John Chambers II, *To Raise an Army: The Draft Comes to Modern America* (1987)

Flynn, George Q., *Conscription and American Culture, 1940-1973* (1992)

Kohn, Stephen M., *Jailed for Peace: The History of American Draft Law Violations, 1658-1985* (1986)

Video:

Conscience and the Constitution (2000). A film by Frank Abe. www.resisters.com

The Good War and Those Who Refused to Fight It (2000). Paradigm Productions, Inc., in association with the Independent Television Service

Government Documents, Reports and Regulations:

Goldrich, Robert L. "The Military Draft and a Possible War With Iraq" December 31, 2002 Congressional Research Service, The Library of Congress

Topical Agenda, February 11, 2003, meeting between officials of the U.S. Department of Defense and the Selective Service System, www.theblatanttruth.org

Original Interviews

Deep thanks to those who took the time to talk about their work: Aimee Allison, Alan Solomonow, Kevin Ramirez, Stephen Funk, Tommi Avicolli Mecca, and Sgt Jemahl Martinson.